Regarding Cocktails

Sasha Petraske
Regarding Cocktails

with Georgette Moger-Petraske

Legend

Liquors

■ ■ Absinthe
■ ■ Amaretto
▪ ▪ Amaro Cio Ciaro
▪ ▪ Amaro Montenegro
▫ ▫ Amaro Nonino
▫ ▫ Aperol
= = Apple brandy
= = Apple liqueur
= = Applejack
≡ ≡ Averna
‖ ‖ Avèze
‖ ‖ Black Strap Rum
‖ ‖ Blanc Vermouth
‖ ‖ Blended Scotch
≡ ‖ Bourbon
◆ ◆ Cachaça
◆ ◆ Campari
◆ ◆ Carpano Antica
◆ ◆ Champagne/prosecco/cava
◇ ◇ Cocchi Americano
◆ ◆ Coffee liqueur
▼ ▼ Cognac
▼ ▼ Curaçao
▼ ▼ Cynar
▼ ▼ Dark rum
▲ ▲ Demerara rum
▲ ▲ Dominican rum

▲ ▲ Dry vermouth
▲ ▲ Elderflower liqueur
✓ ✓ Gin
✓ ✓ Green Chartreuse
�£ �£ Highland whiskey
�£ �£ Islay whiskey
– – Jamaican rum
– – Licor 43
∕ ∕ Maraschino liqueur
∕ ∕ Mezcal
∕ ∕ Orange liqueur
∕ ∕ Pear liqueur
↗ ↘ Pimento dram
∕ ∖ Pisco
∣ – Port
∣ – Punt e Mes
∣ ∣ Red wine
∣ ∣ Rum
∣ ∣ Rye whiskey
∣ ∣ St. Elizabeth Allspice Dram
∣ ∣ Sweet vermouth
▪ ▪ ▪ Tequila blanco
▪ ▪ ▪ Tequila reposado
+ + Triple sec
∴ ∴ Vodka
∴ ∴ White rum
≡ ‖ Yellow Chartreuse

Dairy & Egg

〰 Egg white
● Egg yolk

〜 Heavy cream
〜 Whipped cream

Juices, Sodas, Sweeteners, Bitters

- A.P.P. Bitters
- Angostura bitters
- Apple cider
- Brown sugar cube
- Chocolate bitters
- Club soda
- Demerara sugar cube
- Espresso
- Ginger beer
- Ginger Syrup
- Grapefruit juice
- Grenadine syrup
- Honey
- Honey Syrup
- House Orange Bitters
- Lemon juice
- Lime juice
- Maple syrup
- Mineral Saline
- Orange blossom water
- Orange juice
- Orgeat Syrup
- Peychaud's bitters
- Pineapple juice
- Raspberry preserves
- Rosewater
- Simple Syrup
- Tonic water
- Violette Syrup
- Warm water
- White Peach Purée
- White sugar cube

Garnishes & Muddlers

- Berries
- Blackberry
- Candied ginger
- Cayenne pepper
- Celery
- Cinnamon sticks
- Cloves
- Cocktail cherry
- Cocktail onion
- Cucumber slice
- Grapefruit twist
- Grapefruit wedge
- Grated cinnamon
- Grated nutmeg
- Hot sauce
- Jalapeño slice
- Lemon twist
- Lemon wheel
- Lime wedge
- Lime wheel
- Maraschino cherry
- Mint
- Olive
- Orange twist
- Orange wheel
- Pepper
- Pineapple wedge
- Salt
- Spring onion
- Strawberry
- Worcestershire sauce

Foreword by Dale DeGroff

An old friend who lived in a roomy loft space on Eldridge Street on the Lower East Side of Manhattan was walking his dog one evening late when a crowd of hipsters piled out of the mahjong parlor directly across the street from his entrance. The mahjong parlor was usually frequented by older Chinese men, who smoked heavily and quietly gambled away the family grocery money.
So my friend approached the group and asked them what they were doing in the mahjong parlor. *"Oh no...it is a really cool bar."* My pal went to investigate. He found a serious young man, white-shirted and suspendered, standing behind a very small bar about a third of the way into the long narrow room. The rest of the bar was empty.

Sasha Petraske introduced himself to his neighbor from across the street and Joe added a little stop to his late night dog walk, well, at least for a couple months while it was quiet—after that the pace started to pick up.

That first night, Joe happened to mention his favorite bar, The Promenade Bar in The Rainbow Room, and said he wanted to bring in his pal Dale DeGroff to see the new addition to the neighborhood. Sasha was excited about the prospect, so Joe called me and we went in together a few nights later.

What struck me when I walked in, was how unlike other bars this bar was. I could tell that this guy had a vision but it was a work in progress. There wasn't a garnish tray with the plastic inserts like the one that sits on a thousand bars around town, instead Sasha had fabricated an attractive stainless steel box. The box was maybe two feet long and a foot wide and had a perforated stainless steel insert about halfway up the inside of the box, upon which crushed ice was neatly packed, and on top of the ice was a variety of fruits. My next trip in I gave Sasha two books, a Trader Vic's drink book and *The Old Waldorf-Astoria Bar Book*, and he used them!

Sasha hit me with question after question. What sort of ice did I use? *"Kold-Draft large cubes and Kold-Draft crushed."* I had both machines, the largest one Kold-Draft made at the time. No way he could afford those, he gave me the blow-by-blow how he had built the place on a shoestring budget. He occasionally hired some cheap neighborhood help. Sasha met his future partner Richie Boccato that way.

Sasha was a problem solver. He bought a large second hand freezer for nothing and started making his own ice in pans. It gave him the ability to make the cubes any size he wanted. Then he bought a used small freezer, which he installed behind the bar to keep not only the ice but the glass part of the Boston shakers in which he assembled the drink ingredients.

I told him that when I made my sour drinks I always assembled in a mixing glass by adding the sour ingredient, followed by the sweet ingredient, followed by the dashes and splashes, and then the base alcohol, and only then would I add the ice. I was a free pour bar and I needed to do this to get consistency. He pondered and decided. #1 He would follow that order. #2 He would never free pour but always use a jigger. #3 Finally after futzing with the frozen glass parts of the shaker assembly he decided that what he needed was all metal Boston shakers sets to achieve the coldest drink possible. That idea has galvanized the bar tool business and every young craft bartender in the business uses metal on metal now. Sasha was never a follower.

"The speakeasy idea was an accident," Sasha announced to me one day over the bar. *"I never wanted to lock my doors, but despite my best efforts and entreaties someone wrote about the place and the numbers doubled and then quadrupled, the flood gates opened. I locked the doors."* Some of us got keys. Others were buzzed in and then he realized that it had to be by reservation only. All this because Sasha wanted to be a good neighbor to the Chinese brethren living above and around the joint.

Sasha named his bar Milk & Honey, an imaginary place of plenty. He led us out of the wilderness to a place where soft-spoken bartenders solicit your favorite spirits and flavors in a effort to craft a perfect drink. Sasha got us there, but he won't be joining us for the next round.

All the rest of this amazing, tragically shortened career will be documented by writers more skilled than I, but the man I knew was a deeply caring individual in a profession that often brings out the opposite tendencies in people. He made employees feel like partners and—in fact some became partners. He changed our business profoundly and brought thousands of talented young people to the profession by simply being himself, curious, innovative and a fundamentally decent human being.

Foreword by Robert Simonson

Until about a decade ago, I didn't much enjoy going out to drink.
The average bar conjured up images of louts drinking for its effect,
making what is jocularly referred to in drinking circles as "poor
decisions," and exhibiting the camaraderie that is just bullying.

The bartenders, meanwhile, were indifferent and indolent,
clock punchers who put in minimal effort into the maybe twelve
different orders they regularly answered. Most bars were designed,
it seemed, for people to let off steam. I understood that urge.
But when I went to a bar, my wish was to collect myself and maybe
grasp at a fraying thread of civilized society.

Sasha Petraske was the first bar owner I met who shared
my vision of what adult drinking could be. If pressed to describe
his philosophy of drink-making and bartending in one word,
I could lean on a number of nouns: precision, elegance, sophisti-
cation, simplicity, dedication. But care probably sums it up best.
It extended to his patrons and employees. Milk & Honey was,
in his own words, "a secret oasis of quality in the desert." Good
drinks served by conscientious people to appreciative customers
on their best behavior. That's all he wanted. It was a lot to ask.
The miracle is that he succeeded at all.

His standards are reflected in this charming, personal,
and principled book. There's a lot to learn here beyond how to
make a good cocktail.

Some years after Milk & Honey asserted its influence,
a younger breed of mixologists rebelled and began opening
more casual cocktail bars, with louder music and a more raucous
atmosphere. It was an effort to get back to the idea that bars were
supposed to be about having a "good time."

But there are all kinds of good times. Sasha gave us one
of the best.

Introduction
by Georgette Moger-Petraske

"As far as I know, there has never been a book detailing the practical logistics of bartending home parties, nor any primers on large-format ice going into any detail on shaking or stirring rather than just straining over it." It was my husband's intent to create a how-to guide, sharing particulars for cocktail preparation at the professional level. Aesthetically, it was to be a minimalist's guide to mixing Milk & Honey-quality drinks at home. Barring one exception, Sasha's essay on Cocktails for Cats (page 251), it was going to be a serious book tantamount to *The Savoy Cocktail Book* by Harry Craddock, (Constable & Company, Ltd., 1930).

My husband was far from finished writing his book when our families of blood and bond felt the gravity of his loss. But Sasha's legacy was too important—and his essays, guidelines, and guidance too great a treasure—for cocktail enthusiasts to never see. Sasha's recipes, and others created by members of the Milk & Honey family, are contained within these pages, as are personal stories about technique, posture, style, how the cocktails came to be, and our own customs of traveling and entertaining with cocktails during our time together.

This guide eschews photos of backlit cocktails, and soft-focused cuffs high-pouring into crystal coupes. In its place, a new order with clean illustrations that focus on the drink components themselves, and a bookmark legend serve as guides, to demystify cocktail making, even for the novice. It only seemed right that this degree of Sasha's method-making professionalism and mad-professor brilliance would serve as our template.

The form this book has taken is one my husband could never have foreseen. Being the subject rather than the narrator would not have been for him, and the book surely contains more of

Sasha's personality than he wished for it to have—but how could it not? A book published posthumously speaks intimately to the reader; it reflects as it instructs. Throughout *Regarding Cocktails*, it has been my ultimate intention to keep Sasha's voice ever present.

> The falcon cannot hear the falconer;
> Things fall apart; the centre cannot hold;
> ... Surely some revelation is at hand; ...
> —William Butler Yeats, "The Second Coming"

With Sasha's last bar endeavor, The Falconer (now rechristened Seaborne), he aimed to return to the simplicity of the first Milk & Honey. The success of his first bar on Eldridge Street on the Lower East Side of Manhattan spawned many imitators, but he was humbled that cocktails had finally been elevated from the state they had been in—at best, made only of two components; at worst, lackluster concoctions served in room-temperature glassware. When most people were reaching for concentrate or pre-batched citrus, he incorporated a juice *à la minute* program at his bar. He didn't expect an entire culture to be built on cocktails. It wasn't like that at all in the early days of M&H. Guests ordering a bartender's choice would specify what spirit base they would like. From there, they would simply be asked—stirred and straightforward? Something refreshing over ice? When served, cocktails would be presented by their names only, not with a rundown of every ingredient they contained. "The drink is dying," Sasha would say, "the longer you keep it from being consumed."

Sasha taught that just about every cocktail was a variation of one of five types of drinks: the Old Fashioned, the Martini or Manhattan, the Sour, the Highball, or the Fix. Therefore, *Regarding Cocktails* is organized into five drink chapters reflecting this, with an additional chapter on punches, flips, and dessert and temperance cocktails for teetotalers.

Setting Up

The Home Cocktail Bar

There are many scales of a home cocktail bar, from freestanding carts or other furniture to a dedicated shelf or two in a kitchen cabinet or bookcase, and all the way down to the smallest plan, which is to have one's portable bar kit to hand.

Glassware

Minimally you will need at least eight each of the following glasses: Cocktail (4 to 6 oz / 120 to 180 ml), Old Fashioned (10 to 12 oz / 300 to 360 ml), and Collins/Highball (11 to 13 oz / 330 to 390 ml). It is also a good idea to have eight wine glasses (a 12-oz / 360 ml Bordeaux is versatile), and it is a pleasing indulgence to spend a bit of money on some heavy, beautiful neat whiskey glasses (5 to 9 oz / 150 to 270 ml). Eschew the brandy snifter in favor of brandy tasting glasses. With a bit of looking, one can find a single port glass that can wear many hats: for port, sherry, or amaro. At thrift stores and yard sales, one may find antique cocktail glasses, usually 2 to 3 oz (60 to 90 ml) in volume, which are a wonderful way to imbibe, but of course make for more work for the bartender.

Disposable Servingware: Feline and Human

Here we find a convenient dividing line between serving drinks and treats at home to a few friends and a full-on party. Do not consider disposable cups and bowls unless the scale of the party allows for no other option, or if you are serving only cats.

Checklist of Equipment for the Home Bar

Required
Juicer, manual
Mixing glasses, 16-oz (480 ml): 3
Large cocktail shakers: 3
Small cocktail shakers: 3
Hawthorne strainers: 2
Julep strainer
Muddler
Cutting board
Serrated knife for citrus
Paper towels for cleanup
Spray bottle of glass cleaner
Hand-washing soap (I recommend Dr.Bronner's unscented
    hand soap, diluted with water 1:4)
Carafe for drinking water
Tablespoon
Jiggers, at least one of each: ½-oz (15 ml), ¾-oz (22 ml),
    and 1½-oz (45 ml)
Swiss peeler
Green scrubby pad
Empty bottles and/or small pitchers for juices and syrups: 6
Salt shaker
Pepper mill
Aerator for cat cocktails
N2O cartridges for aerator

Optional
Nutmeg grater
Cinnamon grater
Egg separator

Checklist of Garnishes and Fruit for the Home Bar

Required
   Candied ginger
   Olives in brine, chilled
      (I recommend Cerignola or Castelveltrano)
   Luxardo Maraschino cherries
      (pronounced "mar-as-KEEN-o")
   Orange and lemons (for peels)
   Seedless (Hothouse) cucumber
   Berries in season
   Mint, whole sprigs in ice water
   Mint leaves, stripped for shaking

Optional
   Cayenne pepper
   Chile flakes
   Rosewater
   Orange blossom water
   Absinthe in a spray bottle
   Cinnamon sticks
   Nutmeg berries
   Pineapple
   Green apple
   Celery stalk
   Fish flakes, for cat cocktails

Checklist of Syrups and Other Ingredients

Simple Syrup (page 20)
Violette Syrup (page 20)
Ginger Syrup (page 21)
Honey Syrup (page 21)
Orgeat Syrup (page 22)
Mineral Saline (page 23)
A.P.P. Bitters (page 23)
House Orange Bitters (page 24)
Grenadine syrup
Coco Lopez
Heavy cream
Medium eggs, cagefree and shells washed with soap
Club soda, ice-cold (minimum 4 bottles on ice, case in fridge)

Simple Syrup

Makes 1 cup (240 ml)

½ cup (100 g) granulated sugar
½ cup (120 ml) filtered water

Combine the sugar and water in a container and stir until the
sugar is completely dissolved. Do not boil, as many recipes
instruct, as that would cause some of the liquid to evaporate
and skew your water content when making cocktails. Cover
and refrigerate for up to 4 days.

Violette Syrup

Makes ½ cup (120 ml)

2 oz (60 ml) gin
1 oz (30 ml) violet syrup, such as Monin
1 oz (30 ml) Simple Syrup (recipe above)

Combine the gin, violet syrup, and simple syrup in a
non-reactive container and stir until well blended. Cover and
refrigerate for up to 1 month.

Ginger Syrup

Makes 1 cup (240 ml)

½ cup (120 ml) fresh ginger juice
½ cup (100 g) superfine sugar

Combine the juice and sugar in a non-reactive container and stir until the sugar is completely dissolved. Cover and refrigerate for up to 5 days.

Honey Syrup

Makes 1⅓ cups (320 ml)

1 cup (240 ml) honey
⅓ cup (80 ml) hot water

Combine the honey and water in a container and stir until well blended. Cover and refrigerate for up to 5 days.

Orgeat Syrup

Makes 1 ¼ cups (300 ml)

2 cups (220 g) toasted slivered almonds
1 ½ cups (300 g) granulated sugar
1 ¼ cups (200 ml) water
1 oz (30 ml) vodka
1 teaspoon orange flower water

Grind the almonds in a food processor, to a coarse powder. Combine the sugar and water in a medium saucepan and bring to a boil over medium-low heat. Cook, stirring constantly, for 3 minutes until sugar dissolves. Add the almonds and continue stirring for an additional 3 minutes. Remove from the heat, cover, and let the syrup sit for 6 hours.

Transfer the syrup to a jelly bag. Squeeze the syrup into a spouted measuring cup, add the vodka and orange flower water, and stir to combine. Cover and refrigerate for up to 1 month.

Mineral Saline

Makes 5 cups (about 1.2 L)

½ cup (68 g) kosher salt
4½ cups (1 L) mineral water, warmed

Combine the salt and mineral water in a nonreactive container
and stir until the salt is completely dissolved. Cover and
refrigerated for up to 1 month.

A.P.P. Bitters

Angostura bitters
Peychaud's bitters
Dale DeGroff's Pimento bitters

Combine equal parts of the three bitters in a nonreactive
container. Cover and store at room temperature indefinitely.

House Orange Bitters

Fee Brothers West Indian Orange bitters
Regan's No. 6 bitters

Combine equal parts of the two bitters in a nonreactive container. Cover and store at room temperature indefinitely.

White Peach Purée

Makes enough for approximately 6 cocktails

1 white peach, skin left on, pitted and sliced
1 oz (30 ml) fresh Meyer lemon juice
1 oz (30 ml) Simple Syrup (page 21)

Combine the peach, lemon juice, and syrup in a small food processor and purée until smooth. Strain through a fine-mesh sieve into a non-reactive jar. Use immediately, or cover and refrigerate for up to 2 days.

The Home Cocktail Party

Some Words on Safety

It is crucial to remember that while it is fine to enjoy a drink or two at one's own party, the safety of your guests is your responsibility and yours alone. This means that if you are going to have enough to drink to make driving illegal, you must designate someone else to remain sober. Often, this would be someone hired from a service, or a volunteer from your group of friends. (This person clearly doesn't get to drink at all.) Someone must be able to call an ambulance, God forbid, or drive someone to a hospital, and be cogent enough to make decisions about calling cabs for guests who are in no shape to drive. One cannot make an accurate estimate of someone else's sobriety when one is inebriated oneself.

Step 1: Determine the capacity of your venue, and from that the number of guests and bartending stations.

    The maximum capacity for your house or apartment is not how many people can fit in it without anyone being trampled, but rather how many people can be promptly served and be provided with bathroom facilities. Allowing eight to ten square feet per person is a good starting point. One bathroom can serve forty guests maximum.

    Your invitation should be clear about whether or not people may bring guests without telling you in advance. If it is a relatively informal party and people may be telling any number of friends, it is a good idea to designate a doorman to hold the door when capacity is reached and implement a two-in, two-out policy.

    Once you have determined how many people will be in the place at one time, you can determine how many bars and/or self-service beer and wine or punch stations you should have. One bartender working with batched cocktails and punch, in a well-set-up bar with a clearly visible menu, can serve up to forty guests, maximum. If you make beer and wine a separate self-serve station, that can up the capacity to fifty. And if you add a self-serve punch station you can serve up to sixty people.

If your party is above sixty people, it is quite likely that some of the service will be outside. Self-serve stations can be repeated outside, with a sign that reads "Cocktail Service at the Inside Bar" or something similar.

Step 2: Decide on glassware or plastic.

The next decision to be made once the capacity has been decided on is whether or not you have the dishwashing or storage capacity, plus the inclination, to use real glassware. Depending on the formality of the party, size of the space, and your budget, you may decide to go with plastic cups. If so, it is crucial to find plastic cups that are 9 ounces (267 ml) or under and plastic champagne flutes or saucers for the straight-up cocktails. Using 12- or 16-ounce cups (355 or 474 ml), such as you may remember from your university days, will inevitably result in guests being overserved, and all that implies.

If you are to use real glass, you must determine if you will be washing glasses as you go, allowing each glass to be used only once, or renting enough glassware to allow for several glasses per guest. In a gathering of just a few friends in a small apartment, guests may reuse their glasses when having another of the same drink, but this is obviously an extremely informal situation, barely qualifying for the term "Cocktail Party." To do things properly, you must either have hired help or volunteer dedicated to clearing tables and washing glasses, or rent your glassware—which can be a considerable expense. It is often more than the cost of a dishwasher.

Rented glassware must be arranged days in advance.

It should arrive in 20-x-20-inch (50-x-50 cm) racks, which stack neatly on top of each other. The dirty (but empty) glassware is returned, upright, in these same racks. This means that you need at least 2.75 square feet (0.8 meters) of clear floor space for each type of glass, clean and dirty. If you have three different types of glasses—cocktail, highball, and wine—you will need a roughly 2-x-6-foot (0.6-x-1.6-meter) space for clean glassware at your bar and a similar space elsewhere for the dirty glasses.

Step 3: Make a menu.

At a cocktail bar, there is an immense selection of possibilities, but a limited selection is a must at the home cocktail party. It is simply not possible to have all the necessary ingredients and equipment to go menu-less at home (unless you build a professional, fully-plumbed bar and purchase at least two commercial freezers). The time per drink would also be greatly increased due to the additional time spent talking to each guest about his or her choice of cocktail. Remember: no one enjoys a party where they cannot get a drink. If you are a member of the more-money-than-sense set and have already built such a bar, please carry this folly to its logical conclusion and hire professional bartenders for your party.

The menu should consist of four to six cocktails, plus beer and wine, along with the basic spirit mixers (tonic for a Gin & Tonic, soda for a Whiskey & Soda, etc.). Even if craft cocktails are the centerpiece of the party, these are essential. Believe me, when a limping, grizzled member of the Greatest Generation asks you for a Scotch & Water and you have to admit that you did not think to prepare for such, the offer of a freshly muddled Strawberry Fix will do nothing to help the situation. And it is gross snobbery not to stock the basics of red and white wine and a lager.

Step 4: Select the Glassware—Number and type.

The cocktails selected for the menu will determine the types of glassware needed. The essentials are: a glass that can serve as a water glass, a highball glass for spirits and mixers and long drinks (as well as beer), and a champagne saucer or flute that can double as a cocktail glass.

It is quite possible to serve a far-ranging menu with just these three glasses. In a pinch, wine can be served "peasant-style," in the highball glass, as long as the servers have an example glass with a piece of tape to show the 6-oz (180 ml) mark. Ambiguous portion sizes will inevitably lead to guests being overserved.

A proper rocks glass for whiskey on its own and Old Fashioned–style cocktails is also an option. In a menu of four drinks, one such stirred-down drink is a good idea. Wine glasses are needed for wine above a certain quality. The "All-Purpose Glass" that your local rental company offers, a durable 8 to 10-oz (237 to 296 ml) wine glass with a short stem, is the most efficient option, as it can serve as the highball as well as the water, wine, and beer glass. However, this jack-of-all-trades should only be used for very large events such as weddings or concerts, when nothing else would be practical.

Your menu should include at least one Mocktail and one low-alcohol drink served long over club soda, such as an Americano. People who are driving need such an option in order to pace themselves. Offering an Old Fashioned–style drink and a Martini or Manhattan variation is a good idea for a proper cocktail party, and a combination of the shaken, straight-up category, such as a Daiquiri and a self-serve punch, will do most of the heavy lifting.

If you are renting glassware, assume four drinks per person for a cocktail party or two per person for a "cocktail hour," evenly distributed among the types of glassware offered. Depending on your wine offering and the drinking habits of your guests, add between zero and one-quarter of this total in wine glasses.

Then add more highball glasses to account for water, beer, soda, etc. Renting slightly too many glasses is a necessity, not a waste.

If you will be washing glassware instead of renting, you need two glasses for each guest, calculated as above, and a sink that is not the bartender's sink, plus a drying area. To set up such an area with no plumbing, build a three-compartment plunge sink to lay between two surfaces out of a wood plank, fashioned with three cut-outs for inexpensive sink basins.

Deciding whether to shake batched Daiquiri-style cocktails to order or to ladle out punch is more about manpower than anything else. These two types of drink do the same thing, delivering quite a bit of alcohol in a quick and painless fashion. As any student of cocktail history will tell you though, punch is essentially British and the shaken cocktail indisputably American. So a combination of a bartender shaking drinks and a self-service punch station is probably best.

To determine if self-serve stations are appropriate, two factors should be considered: the possibility of guests overserving themselves and the formality and level of service desired. How large is the party? Is there line-of-sight between the host or a member of staff and the self-serve station? These are the questions to ask in regard to the first consideration. The nightmare scenarios include a guest serving himself too much and causing a tragedy, or the teenage child of your next-door neighbor sneaking past the doorman, getting drunk, and ending up in the coat closet with one of your unsuspecting guests.

As far as for formality, use this as a rule of thumb: Imagine your party in full swing. If the guests serve their own beer, they will drink from the bottle, with a glass being available upon request. If the bartender opens the beer for the guests, it will be poured into a glass unless otherwise requested. If the party is too formal for drinking beer from the bottle, it is too formal for a self-serve station.

Step 5: Set up the bar.

First things first: Where is the running water? The bartender will need a sink to rinse shakers and wash his or her hands, and if there is the possibility of having a real sink, this should determine the placement of your bar. Pass-through kitchens work very well for this sort of thing, with the breakfast bar acting as a very serviceable substitute for the real thing. If there is no pass, pull a folding card table or such up to the entrance to the kitchen, barricading the bartender inside —this gives us the term "barricade bar."

If there is no kitchen available, a set of inexpensive or rented folding tables, covered with tablecloths, can make a bar that will suffice. A gravity-powered slop sink rigged with a sump pump can be a workable substitute for a real sink, and Igloo coolers, raised to an appropriate height on milk crates or something similar, can hold the ice. The tablecloths are not optional—they are needed to cover the stuff that will be stored under the bar, such as dirty-glass racks and garbage cans.

The following three setups are largely the same and share the following features:

1.   Work area: This is a rectangular space approximately 8 inches (20 cm) deep and 24 inches (60 cm) wide upon which the drinks are built. A neatly folded dinner napkin or towel will suffice, or a rubber spill mat or two can be purchased online or from a restaurant supply store. If you already have a well-set-up home bar, use your steel coffee drip tray.

2.   Ice bins: A clean garbage can with a clean liner can store a whole night's worth of bagged ice. Remember, ice keeps ice cold. A small Igloo cooler or set of two stacking Tupperware storage bins should be used for serving the ice along with a second salted

one to store Martini batches. (Adding salt to the ice/water mix, causes a temperature drop, which slows the melting rate. As a result, the ice melts slower.) A third bin is for bottles of drinking water, tonic, soda, and back-up batches of shaken cocktails. The Cadillac of home-bar ice bins is an Igloo cooler with half a block of dry ice cracked in the bottom, but be careful not to get burned! A radiator screen from your local hardware store, trimmed with scissors to fit in the bottom of the cooler, should be placed between the dry ice and the cooler's contents. Spritz some water into the cooler from time to time to activate the dry ice.

3. Garbage and recycling cans with extra bags: Remember to put a colander in your sink so that you can empty all plastic cups and beer bottles before disposing of them. No one likes to get coated with garbage juice when the bag breaks.

4. Glass Froster: For a small (fifteen people or under, say) party, you can use your freezer if the bar is in the kitchen. Otherwise, you have a choice between the dry-ice method described above and what we call the "19th-Century Glass Froster": essentially, cocktail glasses laid out in a grid, with the first row full of ice water and the second and third rows full of ice. Rows four through six (or more, as your counter space and party size dictate) are empty. When you need a glass, transfer the contents to an empty one, briskly shake out any remaining water, and use to serve.

5. Spirits: Your mixing spirits, including empty bottles to represent what is in the batches, should be displayed, label facing out, on either the back or front bar.

6. Menu: A large-format menu, printed or on a chalkboard, will massively speed things up. Imagine yourself listing your complete cocktail and beer offerings to the thirtieth person that night while

a line of people taps their feet impatiently, and you will see what I mean. If a large-format menu is not an option, print many 8 1/2-x-11-inch (22-x-28 cm) ones, with type large enough to read in low light.

7. Paper towels and/or dish towels: More than you think you will need.

8. Dustpan and broom: Have these on hand, along with the empty cardboard tube from a whiskey bottle or something to put broken glass in before throwing it in the recycling bin. This is a must for the safety of whomever takes out the garbage at the end of the night, as well as the garbagemen.

9. Ice scoops, muddlers, bottle openers, and corkscrews: One per bartender.

10. A small bottle each of simple syrup and fresh lemon juice: To adjust drinks to the taste of a particular guest.

11. Bowls: For garnishes, as appropriate.

12. Cutting board, knife, and fruit bowl: With two Swiss peelers. Two, not one.

13. Cocktail shakers: One Hawthorne strainer per shaken cocktail per bar. As these are each dedicated to one cocktail, they will rarely need to be rinsed between uses, just occasionally rinsed on the outside.

14. Carafes: Glass or plastic, to hold batched, shaken cocktails. The backup batches can either be in the refrigerator or freezer or on ice, either in carafes with tops or poured back into the empty liquor bottles used to make them.

15. Teapot or "Penguin"-style large shakers: For stirred, straight-up batched cocktails. Backup batches should be stored in liquor bottles in the freezer, or well surrounded by salted ice and water in the cooler.

16. A 2-oz (60 ml) jigger: For pouring spirits with mixers or rocks.

Step 6: Create ambiance and music.

Ninety percent of creating the right ambiance for a cocktail party is simply dimming the lights. If you don't have dimmers, switching regular bulbs to 7-watt nightlight bulbs (they look like golf balls) for the evening, or shading your lights with translucent fabric or paper, can have a lovely effect. Dim bulbs for the bathrooms are a good idea as well; the intrusion of bright light every time the door opens can throw off the mood. The decision to use candles or not should be based on your estimation of how crazy the party might get. Candles placed on stairs or near curtains can spell disaster.

Moving your valuables, as well as extra furniture and clutter, into the bedroom and locking the door is also a good idea if the party is larger than an intimate gathering of friends.

If your guests are not arriving by car and the weather is cold, extra coat hangers and a folding garment rack (essentially a freestanding closet bar) are a good purchase for a party of any significant size. These are available from Bed, Bath & Beyond and other housewares stores for not too much scratch.

In the summer, be sure to turn the air conditioners on before the party starts to reach capacity. The recommended air-conditioner capacity for a restaurant or bar is 500 Btu per guest, which you are unlikely to have. Home units will probably not catch up with a shoulder-to-shoulder crowd in the summer, which is why you want to give them a head start. In the winter, you can always open a window if it gets too hot.

As far as music goes, it is crucial that you (or the doorman) have control of the volume. In order to change the volume in response to the size of the crowd and placate any irate neighbors, make an announcement if you need to, and lower the music accordingly. I recommend making three playlists—fast, medium, and slow— and being sure that there is not a mediocre song among them. When it is time for the party to start winding down (and not a second before), switch to the slow playlist.

Step 7: How much ice to order?

Eight 5-pound (2.5 kg) bags from the supermarket or one 40-pound (20 kg) bag from an ice delivery service are the norm. For delivery two hours before the party setup starts, order five pounds per guest. The "cheater" or "dice" style ice that super-markets provide is not ideal, but it is usually the only practical option. For a very small party, or if you are truly loaded, large-format Clinebell ice can be purchased, precut into individual blocks and spears, from a commercial ice company such as HundredWeight in New York or Penny Pound in Los Angeles. This option requires tremendous freezer space and is quite costly, but it is just the thing for a certain sort of occasion. If you do order this kind of ice, you will still need standard ice for chilling beer, cocktail ingredients, and ice water.

Step 8: For God's sake, don't forget the bottle openers. Or the corkscrews. This happens more than you might think.

Consider the Peacock
(a note on garnishes)

For some, the very existence of any accoutrements to the simple act of imbibing points to everything that is objectionable and pretentious about cocktails. For others, the cocktail is present evidence of the bartender's competence. For this camp, a poorly executed garnish is a cause for concern.

As is usually the case, both camps are partially correct. Let us first distinguish between traditional garnishes and garnish-as-ingredient, such as the strip of orange peel in an Old Fashioned, or the mint sprig in a Julep. The aromas, and in some cases tastes, of these are crucial to the drink and should thus not be excused from these proceedings. At a basic level, if you don't have citrus peel, you don't bother to make an Old Fashioned.

A case can certainly be made that non-ingredient garnishes are a distraction from the task at hand. One doesn't garnish a glass of Armagnac, for instance. However, for the garnishes that are merely that—such as candied ginger or the raspberry on top of a Raspberry Fix—poor quality or execution are often advance warning that other crucial aspects of the cocktail have been neglected. A sorry, dilapidated blackberry garnish shows a head bartender or bar manager not up to the tasks of ordering and rotating produce. And the best looking of the pint were probably chosen for garnish, so did the blackberries muddled in the drink have a spot of mold?

A scrawny mint sprig shows a bartender either lacking in concern for what he is sending out or overwhelmed by his circumstances. As accurately measuring the lime juice portion of the drink is markedly more difficult than placing the garnish, it is a distinct possibility that the drink will be either too tart or too sweet. The very act of letting a drink go out with a substandard

Setting Up

garnish rather than naked is evidence of being either in the weeds or past caring. Though some may think that a cocktail without garnish is an abomination, I am here to tell you: for a non-ingredient garnish, the bartender always has the option of skipping or replacing the garnish with something else if nothing of acceptable quality is at hand. It better to garnish a Mojito with a lime wedge than with a sad sprig of mint.

It is useful, then, to look at the garnish as a zoologist would a biological ornament. Famously, the Peacock demonstrates his suitability to the Peahen with a breathtaking demonstration of plumage, which indicates that he has had the spare nutrition to divert away from the basic task of keeping Peacock body and Peacock soul together. A bartender who can, even in the thick of it, take the time to select and place the garnish, and who has the presence of mind to correct the inevitable fallen garnish on the fly, is the one you want making your cocktail.

On Frozen Water
by Richard Boccato

Sasha and I often spoke about the subject of ice, and how it can contribute to a successful and exemplary cocktail. These conversations took place sometimes late at night at the bar and in later years, via e-mail, often with thousands of miles of land and ocean between us. Sasha showed me long before my personal "ice capades" that the fundamentals for our approach to mixing drinks with frozen water could always be found in *The Savoy Cocktail Book* by Harry Craddock.

A Few Hints For The Young Mixer.

1. Ice is nearly always an absolute essential for any Cocktail.
2. Never use the same ice twice.
3. Remember that the ingredients mix better in a shaker rather larger than is necessary to contain them.
4. Shake the shaker as hard as you can: don't just rock it: you are trying to wake it up, not send it to sleep!
5. If possible, ice your glasses before using them.
6. Drink your Cocktail as soon as possible. Harry Craddock was once asked what was the best way to drink a Cocktail. "Quickly," replied that great man, "while it's laughing at you!"

The following are Sasha's own words on the role of frozen water and how it affects a cocktail when made the Petraske way.

On temperature as it is governed by ice in a drink:
"I believe that temperature and mouthfeel are as important as the recipe in a cocktail. I often use the following example: Imagine it's

Setting Up

a hot summer day and you've been working outdoors. You crack open an ice-cold bottle of Coke. Unbeatable. Now, leave that same bottle of Coke open at room temperature until it's warm and flat. Undrinkable. Yet we haven't changed the recipe or the chemical composition of it at all."

On why we keep our service ice in the freezer before introducing it into a shaker or mixing glass:
"The temperature of the ice is the most important factor. More specifically, that the ice is dry. The majority of the energy transfer comes at the point of phase change, when the ice becomes water. If the ice is even slightly wet, you are adding water and ice, not just ice. There is some transfer of heat aside from the melting, but not much."

On why we shake with large ice:
"All other things being equal, the advantage to shaking with a big cube is that you can shake longer, giving us the consistency of ice crystals we want on top of the straight-up cocktail. Of course the big cube must break toward the end of the shake for this to work. If it's just "thukka thukka thukka" the whole time, the drink won't be cold enough, or have the head. Another way to save lots of time is to use a frozen spirit: 4 Kold-Draft cubes and frozen rum equals our Daiquiri in every way."

On the target temperature(s) for our cocktails:
"-8°C(18°F) is not realistic. I like -4°C (25°F)—there is a "sweet spot" for every glass size and shape, a temperature at which the drink will stay cold for 20 minutes or so."

On "dilution" versus water content and ABV percentage (alcohol by volume) of a cocktail:
"It doesn't strike me as upsetting that certain cocktails can take

more or less water than others, but I believe it is a relatively narrow range, around 15 to 18 percent for a straight-up citrus-based cocktail. Any drink served on ice, of course, will have a varied water content during its consumption, and the speed with which one consumes a cocktail on ice is certainly in proportion to the surface area of said ice. I think that it is important to make sure that we are talking about an end result, rather than a combination of process and result. I don't like the term 'dilution' for that reason. The water content of a finished cocktail is best expressed as ABV. It doesn't matter at all how the water was added, just how much is in the finished product. Our Daiquiri, I believe, is about 17 percent."

And, therefore:
"We must stop overgeneralizing about water content in cocktails, and instead start speaking in terms of ABV. Calculate the total amount of ethyl alcohol: 0.8 oz (23 ml) for 2 oz (60 ml) 80-proof rum, 0.86 oz (25 ml) for 2 oz (60 ml) 43-proof gin, etc. Divide this by the final volume—this is your ABV percentage."

Per Sasha's instructions, calculate the ABV percentage of a finished cocktail by dividing the total amount of alcohol by the final liquid volume of said cocktail, after shaking with ice to add water content (and achieve optimal temperature).

To calculate the ABV percentage of a shaken Daiquiri with 2 oz (60 ml) 80-proof rum, an initial liquid volume of 3.75 oz (11 ml) prior to shaking with ice, and a final liquid volume of 4.5 oz (133 ml), after introducing water by shaking with ice, to be served in a coupe glass with a total capacity of 5.5 oz (163 ml), the formula would be: 0.8 ÷ 4.5 = 17% ABV

Although it is common for professional bartenders and laypeople to say that a properly mixed cocktail should include approximately

25 to 30 percent water from ice, that stringent universalism should not be arbitrarily applied across the board. All things considered, one need only be concerned with balance, temperature, and water content every time he or she sets forth to prepare a drink, be it a Daiquiri, a Manhattan, an Old Fashioned, or what have you.

At Milk & Honey, Little Branch, and everywhere else where Sasha presided over the bar, he taught us to shake or stir with ice in a way that would allow us to achieve the proper washlines for the specific glass that we were using for each particular cocktail. (The term "washline" refers to the point a poured cocktail reaches on the wall of a glass, leaving a small window of space between the drink and the rim. A glass served full to the brim is generally not a good example of a desired washline.)

We were never to shake or stir our drinks to hit a target washline with a ritualistic and theatrical snap of the wrist— leaving residual water content in the shaker or the mixing glass. Never! If anything, Sasha taught us to make the shaker or glass fit the finished drink, not the other way around. Always good to the last drop.

So, it is imperative that the working bartender exercise care in order to consistently hit the correct ABV, temperature mark, and washline without leaving liquid in the shaker or mixing glass to be discreetly poured down the drain when the boss isn't looking. Same goes for the home bartender entertaining guests.

The last words that Sasha ever wrote to me on this topic were, "Sad to say, we're the only people out there who consider water content a variable to be controlled, rather than a box to be checked: 'Did you get your dilution?' I will not, and you should not, spend one minute of our time on this earth being concerned with these folks. If someone puts up undrinkable drinks when they are bartending, his off-work data is severely compromised when tested in a controlled situation. This is like the 1890s land rush in the west, and we're not gonna throw away our head start."

Recipes

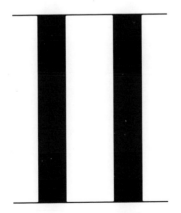

The Old Fashioned

Built-in-the-Glass Cocktails

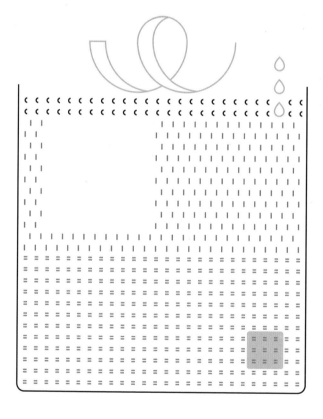

The American Trilogy

During my early training behind the bar at Little Branch and Milk & Honey, I was fortunate enough to share many shifts with Michael McIlroy, whose friendship and tutelage in the ways of the Petraske method of drink-making were fundamental to my career. Once, in the midst of a sleepy shift at Little Branch, I asked Mickey whether or not a cocktail could be built in the glass and devised with ingredients that were slightly different from those that we used to make our house Old Fashioned.

This drink came about without much trial and error, and we gave it the name it still bears. Although the cocktail's contents may not technically be 100 percent "American," neither are the two bartenders who married it in a glass. Apples and oranges, as they say.

—Richard Boccato

1 small brown sugar cube
2 to 4 dashes orange bitters
Splash of club soda
1 oz (30 ml) rye whiskey
1 oz (30 ml) bonded applejack
An orange twist, for garnish

Put the sugar cube in a room-temperature whiskey glass and saturate it with the bitters. Add a splash no bigger than a bar spoon of club soda and gently muddle to make a slightly granular paste. Add the whiskey, applejack, and 1 large ice cube. Stir 10 to 15 times and garnish with the orange twist.

The Old Fashioned

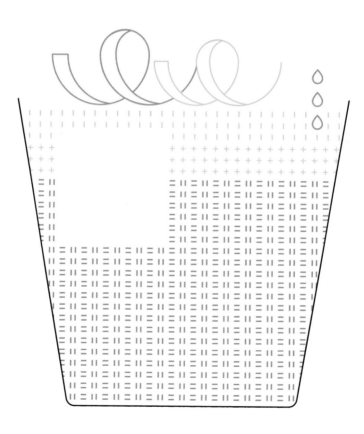

Home on the Range

This drink is based on an old recipe I found years ago in *Crosby Gaige's Cocktail Guide and Ladies' Companion* (M. Barrows and Company, January 1941). The book was a trusted resource to build drinks upon, and Sasha made certain this one made its way to all of his cocktail branches.

—Michael Madrusan

3 dashes Angostura bitters
¼ oz (7.5 ml) sweet vermouth, preferably Cocchi Vermouth
    di Torino
¼ oz (7.5 ml) Cointreau
2 ounces (60 ml) bourbon
A lemon twist, for garnish
An orange twist, for garnish

Build the drink in a rocks glass, starting with the bitters and ending with the bourbon. Add 1 large ice cube and stir a few times. Garnish with the lemon and orange twists.

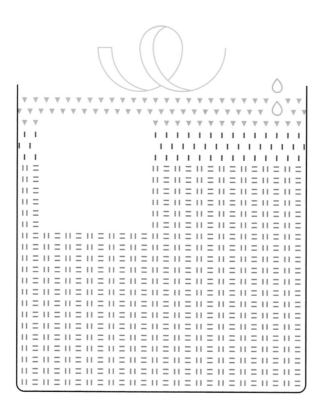

The Sherpa

I met Sasha when I was the doorman at Dutch Kills. Over the course of the next six years, as I worked my way up to bartender, his guidance was invaluable. He was my mentor and a good friend. He always spoke to me as a peer, even at the very beginning of my career. At the time, I remember being exasperated by his meticulousness—we spent nearly an hour and a half adjusting this recipe incrementally in different directions to see what worked best, and in the end we settled on the first recipe we'd tried.

But the experience of trying each minor variation taught me just how delicate the human palate is and just how important it is to be exact in your measurements.

—Matt Clark

2 dashes orange bitters
¼ oz (7.5 ml) Curaçao
¼ oz (7.5 ml) St. Elizabeth Allspice Dram
2 oz (60 ml) bourbon, preferably Elijah Craig 12-year-old
A lemon twist, for garnish

Build the drink in a whiskey glass, starting with the bitters and ending with the bourbon; add a large cube of ice and stir a few times. Since this is a sipping drink, it should have a minimal amount of water content to start, as you want to be able to savor it over time without it becoming too watery. Garnish with the lemon twist.

The Old Fashioned

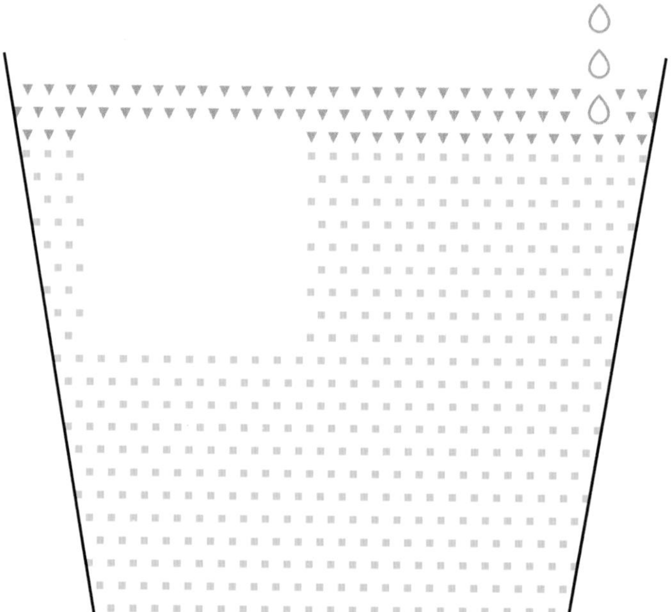

Si-Güey

Segue—as in "to move, without interruption, from one scene to another"—is imperative for working in the tight quarters of any Petraske bar. *Güey* is the colloquial Mexican Spanish way of referring to any person without using his name, and *Sí, Güey,* was something Sasha and all the bartenders would say to one another at various points of the evening.

—Michael Madrusan

3 dashes orange bitters
¼ oz (7.5 ml) Curaçao
2 oz (60 ml) tequila reposado
¼ oz (7.5 ml) Islay whisky

Build the drink in a whiskey glass, starting with the bitters and ending with tequila. Add 1 large ice cube and stir. Finish with a float of the whisky.

The Old Fashioned

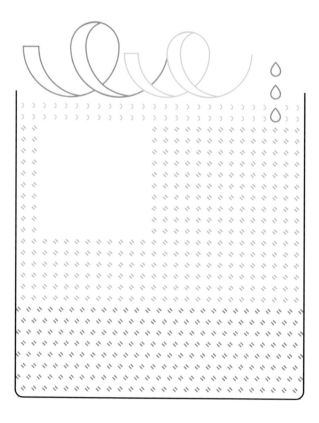

Tattletale

Sasha was more than just a mentor to me; he was one of my closest friends. He was the only one who could come into the bar and bust my chops about washlines, water content, or inefficient jigger use, and you know what?—he was always right. Sasha was thoughtful, gentle, and trusting.

He would come in to Pegu Club when it first opened—it was one of three bars I was working at during that time. I wanted him to try this cocktail, despite the fact that he hated smoky Scotch. He put the glass to his lips and sat up straight. I took one look at his face before removing the offending drink and honoring his request for a double Queen's Park Swizzle (page 197). This cocktail is a deliciously smoky riff on an Old Fashioned, fattened up by using honey instead of sugar.

—Sam Ross

3 dashes Angostura bitters
1 bar spoon honey
1¼ oz (37.5 ml) Highland Scotch
¾ oz (22 ml) Islay whisky
A lemon twist, for garnish
An orange twist, for garnish

Build the drink in a room-temperature whiskey glass, starting with the bitters and ending with the whisky. Add 1 rock ice cube and stir 5 or 6 times. Garnish with the lemon and orange twists.

The Old Fashioned

The Martini and the Manhattan

Cocktails Stirred and Served Up

.38 Special

Sasha wouldn't initally let me name this the .38 Special because
he said it sounded too violent. I had explained the relevance of the
name in regards to the spec, but he wouldn't budge. I brought up
the French 75 (page 161), and he still wouldn't cave. I sulked like
a child, and I rarely made the drink until he'd forgotten about it.
About a month later, he came around.

—Michael Madrusan

2 ⅜ oz (67.5 ml) blended Scotch
⅜ oz (11 ml) yellow Chartreuse
⅜ oz (11 ml) Amaro CioCiaro
A lemon twist, for garnish

Combine the Scotch, Chartreuse, and amaro in a mixing glass
filled with ice and stir until the drink is sufficiently chilled. Strain
into a chilled coupe and garnish with the lemon twist.

The Martini and the Manhattan

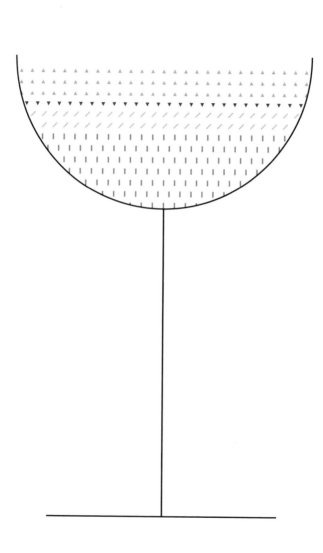

Bensonhurst

I was inspired to create the Bensonhurst as an alternative to the
Brooklyn Cocktail, partly because of the lack of original-formula
Amer Picon. It was the winter of 2006 and I was working at both
Milk & Honey and the Pegu Club. Vincenzo Errico had already
created the Red Hook (page 73) at Milk & Honey in 2004 as the first
of the Brooklyn variations, which set the precedent of choosing
other Brooklyn neighborhoods to name the variations it spawned.

—Chad Solomon

1 oz (30 ml) dry vermouth, preferably Dolin
1 teaspoon (5 ml) Cynar
2 teaspoons (10 ml) Maraschino liqueur, preferably Luxardo
2 oz (60 ml) rye whiskey, preferably Rittenhouse

Combine the vermouth, Cynar, Maraschino liqueur, and whiskey
in a frozen mixing glass and top off with ice. Stir until the drink
is sufficiently chilled, then strain into a frozen coupe.

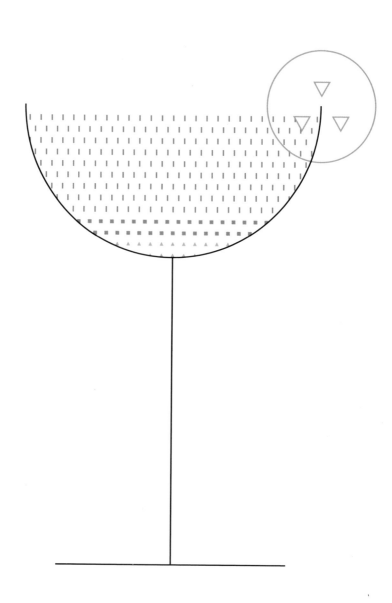

Cobble Hill

This is a very early Milk & Honey drink from when we were putting cucumbers in everything. Sasha and I were thinking of a Manhattan that you could drink during the summertime. We came up with the Cobble Hill—light and floral, as opposed to the heavy style of the classic Manhattan.

—Sam Ross

3 thin cucumber slices
2 oz (60 ml) rye whiskey
½ oz (15 ml) Amaro Montenegro
½ oz (15 ml) dry vermouth

Add 2 cucumber slices to a mixing glass and gently bruise with a muddler. Add the rye, amaro, and vermouth, fill the glass with ice, and stir for 30 seconds. Strain into a chilled coupe and garnish with the remaining cucumber slice.

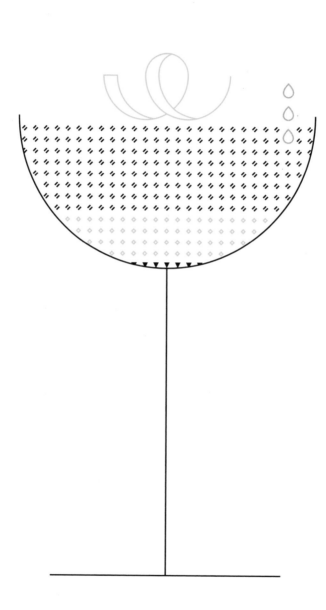

Deep Blue Sea

This was the first drink I created for Sasha. I made the drink so many times, and tried seemingly every variation by the end of the evening, before he finally passed it. (You had to have your drinks approved before you could serve them.) I couldn't believe how much time he gave me that night—it was like Dad playing catch with you.

—Michael Madrusan

2 oz (60 ml) gin
¾ oz (22 ml) Cocchi Americano
¼ oz (7.5 ml) Violette Syrup (page 20)
2 dashes orange bitters
A lemon twist, for garnish

Combine the gin, Cocchi Americano, violette syrup, and bitters in a mixing glass filled with ice. Stir until the drink is sufficiently chilled. Strain into a frozen coupe and garnish with the lemon twist.

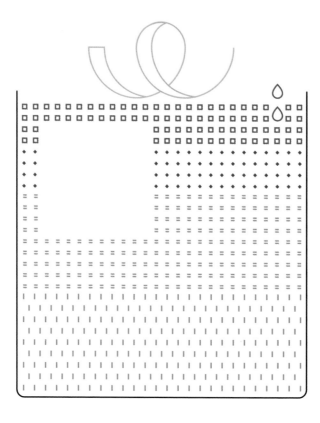

Fallback Cocktail

Sasha created this cocktail for the autumn menu at the John Dory Oyster Bar, where he consulted. It's the perfect indulgence to savor with the guilty pleasure of their buttery Parker House rolls.

—Lucinda Sterling

2 dashes Peychaud's bitters
½ oz (15 ml) Amaro Nonino
½ oz (15 ml) Carpano Antica
1 oz (30 ml) applejack
1 oz (30 ml) rye whiskey
An orange twist, for garnish

Build the drink in a whiskey glass, adding the bitters, amaro, Carpano Antica, applejack, and whiskey. Add 1 large cube, stir until the drink is sufficiently chilled and garnish with the orange twist.

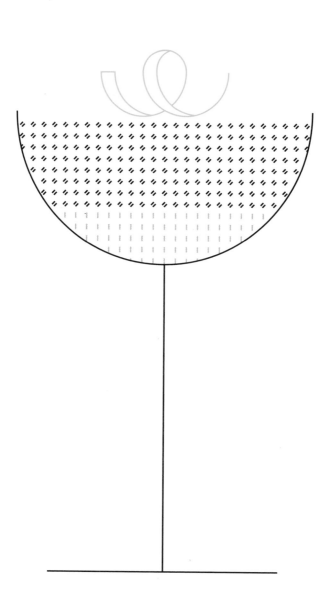

Gin & It

This is right up there with The Business (page 85); I can't think of a cocktail that is more expressly my husband. We both loved this drink so much that we batched it into Mason jars and gave them out as our wedding favors with Milk & Honey coupes. Originally this cocktail was sipped at room temperature. Adding ice to chill and increase water content is a contemporary evolution, and this method has now fallen into favor.

"It" is short for Italian vermouth, and the original recipe from the 1905 *Hoffman House Bartender's Guide: How to Open a Saloon and Make it Pay* (R.K. Fox, January 1905) calls for 2 1/2 ounces gin and 1/2 ounce sweet Italian vermouth, but Sasha and I only ever drank it with a 2:1 gin-to-vermouth ratio.

—Georgette Moger-Petraske

2 oz (60 ml) gin
1 oz (30 ml) sweet vermouth
A lemon twist, for garnish

Stir the gin and vermouth in an ice-filled mixing glass until sufficiently chilled. Strain into a chilled coupe. Twist the lemon peel over the glass to extract the oils, then garnish the drink with the twist.

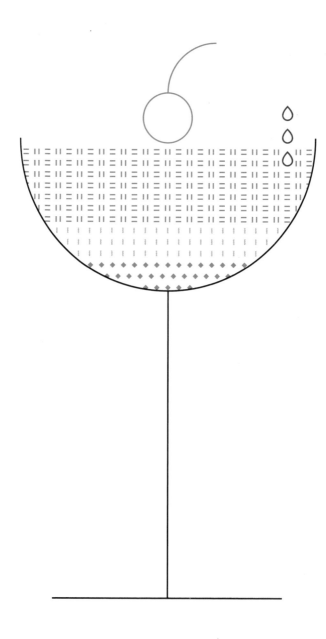

Left Hand

We created a series of "Hand" cocktails in the early days of Milk & Honey. The Right Hand was an aged-rum take; Tres Hands was its mezcal and tequila sister; and the Smoking Hand was her brother from Islay and the Highlands. Before the Boulevardier came back into prominence, this was a bourbon riff on the Negroni that we created using the newly released chocolate bitters from Bittermen's. Sasha reserved his compliments for only a few drinks, but this was one of our cocktails in the "Hand" series that he loved. "Well played, Sam," he said.

—Sam Ross

1½ oz (45 ml) bourbon
¾ oz (22 ml) sweet vermouth
¾ oz (22 ml) Campari
3 dashes Bittermen's chocolate bitters
A brandied cherry, for garnish

Add the bourbon, vermouth, Campari, and bitters to a mixing glass, fill it with ice, and stir for 30 seconds. Strain into a chilled coupe and garnish with the brandied cherry.

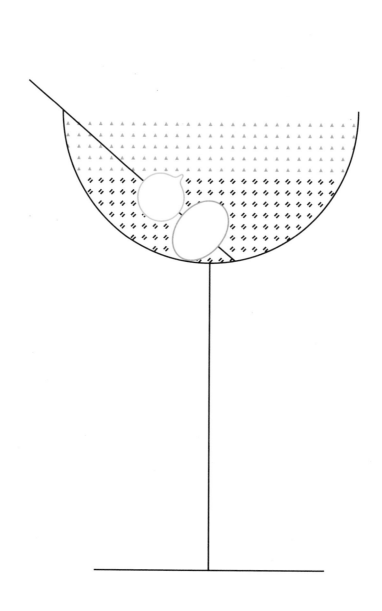

Martini

The Martini is to a stirred drink what a Daiquiri is to a shaken one—total simplicity; just straightforward technique and execution. Conventional wisdom would have you believe that a proper martini is dry, but Sasha's martini was as wet as I've ever seen—a straight 2:1 ratio, and with gin unless otherwise specified.

At the Petraske bars, stirred drinks are, as a rule, built to 3-ounce liquid volume. You would often see Sasha bent low, inspecting the washlines of each round of drinks that were about to go out. He always said that the end goals were a drink that was as cold as possible ("no such thing as a too-cold drink") and the appropriate water content.

All classic Martini garnishes complement the drink, and a lemon twist, potently aromatic and bitter, has to be applied with a light touch. Once I saw Sasha order a Martini with a twist from one of his bartenders, and the bartender squeezed every bit of oil from the twist over the drink. Sasha tasted it and handed it back for him to taste. All you could taste and smell, he said, was the lemon peel, all the balance gone. He wasn't mad or mean about it—just teaching, as always.

—Abraham Hawkins

1 oz (30 ml) dry vermouth
2 oz (60 ml) gin
An olive, a cocktail onion, or a lemon twist, for garnish

Combine the vermouth and gin in a frozen mixing glass. Fill to the top with ice and stir until the drink is sufficiently chilled. Strain into a chilled coupe and garnish with the olive, cocktail onion, or lemon twist.

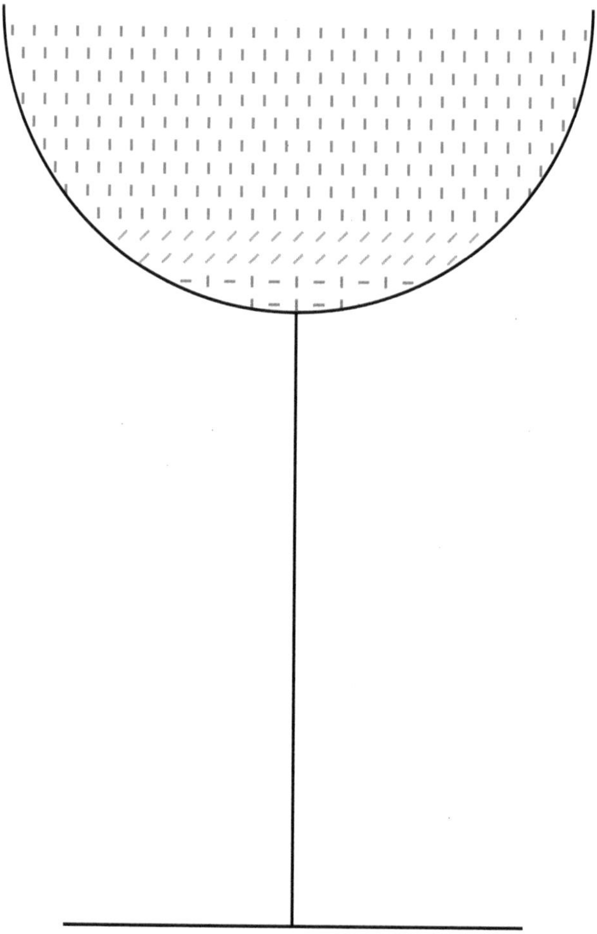

Red Hook Cocktail

I was working at Match Bar in London when I met Sasha for the first time. He had come over to open Milk & Honey London with Jonathan Downey (the owner of the Match company), and I was going to be part of the opening team.

One night I had to pour a glass of Champagne, and I did it holding the bottle with the label facing down. Sasha gently corrected me: the label of the bottle always has to face up when you are serving it. I countered that while I knew that, no one in the bar could see us in there, but he said that it was out of the respect for the product that we had to do it. Such a gentleman always—in and out of the bar.

Later Sasha asked me to work for him at the original Milk & Honey in New York. For me, the original location was the best bar, but not for Sasha. He was always thinking about how he could improve the service. For example, the bartenders there were juicing the citrus for the cocktails to order so the juice wasn't too oxidized. Genius.

I created the Red Hook Cocktail at Milk & Honey in 2003, and I'm proud that this cocktail is now on the menus of many other bars, where it arrived simply by word of mouth.

—Vincenzo Errico

2 oz (60 ml) rye whiskey
½ oz (15 ml) Maraschino liqueur, preferably Luxardo
½ oz (15 ml) Punt e Mes vermouth

Combine the whiskey, Maraschino liqueur, and vermouth in a mixing glass filled with ice and stir until the drink is sufficiently chilled. Strain into a chilled coupe.

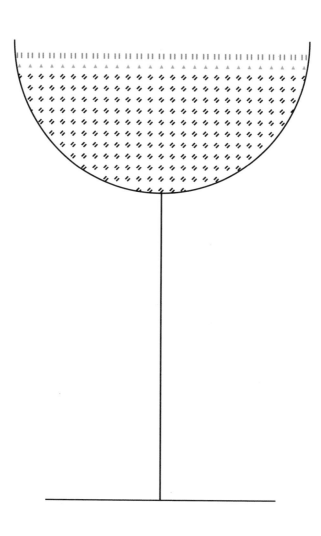

Savoir Faire

Theo Lieberman brought me on to Lantern's Keep where he was the head bartender and held a true reverence for how much care Sasha had put into understanding cocktails. He emphasized that we really needed to live up to that. When the 23rd Street Milk & Honey opened and Theo became the head bartender, he brought me over to work as a bartender. Whenever Sasha would point something out to me or give me a complimentary nod, I felt lucky. He knew that we were all really proud to be there.

Georgette would come to Milk & Honey on 23rd Street to have the occasional cocktail, and I was told that she was a lover of floral drinks. I am also one of those happy few, and I finally got up the guts to make her one of my own cocktails, the Savoir Faire.

—Lauren McLaughlin

¼ oz (7.5 ml) Avèze
¼ oz (7.5 ml) dry vermouth, preferably Dolin
2 oz (60 ml) gin
Orange blossom water, for spraying
A lemon twist, for garnish

Combine the Avèze, vermouth, and gin in a chilled mixing glass filled with cracked ice and stir until ice cold. Lightly spray a frosted coupe with orange blossom water. Strain the cocktail into the coupe. Lightly twist the lemon peel over the cocktail to extract the oils and gently rub the rim of the glass with it, then discard the twist.

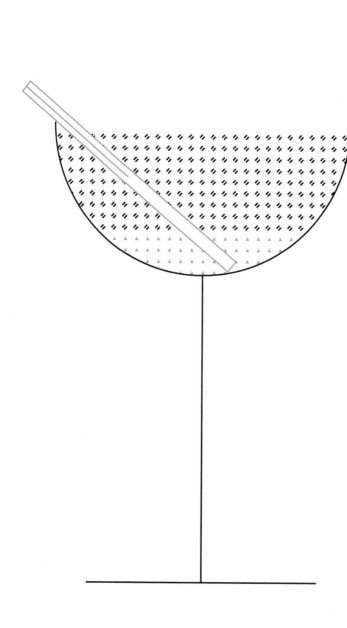

Spring Forward

The Sam Ross and Michael McKillroy Sunday night shift on
Eldridge Street at Milk & Honey was the most "industry" thing
I could have hoped to become a part of. Sasha had assembled
what I thought to be the most amazing bar family in the world.
Sammy was quick to introduce me to Sasha, a quiet but larger-
than-life figure, "Have you met Theo? He is going to be a big part
of our community." Sasha was having a classic riff on the Mai-Tai
that Sam had found in a book. I ordered one as well and resumed
my nervous conversation with the man I had spent months
admiring from afar.

Later that year Sasha told me about a project he was
working on in the Ace Hotel—The John Dory Oyster Bar. This
cocktail is a big seller there.

—Theo Lieberman

2 oz (60 ml) gin
1 oz (30 ml) dry vermouth
2 spring onions or ramps, trimmed

Combine the gin, vermouth, and 1 spring onion in a frozen
mixing glass and gently muddle the onion briefly.
(Overmuddling will result in a bitter flavor.) Fill the glass with
ice and stir until the drink is sufficiently chilled. Strain into
a chilled coupe and garnish with the remaining spring onion.

The Martini and the Manhattan

The Sour

Traditional and Non-Traditional

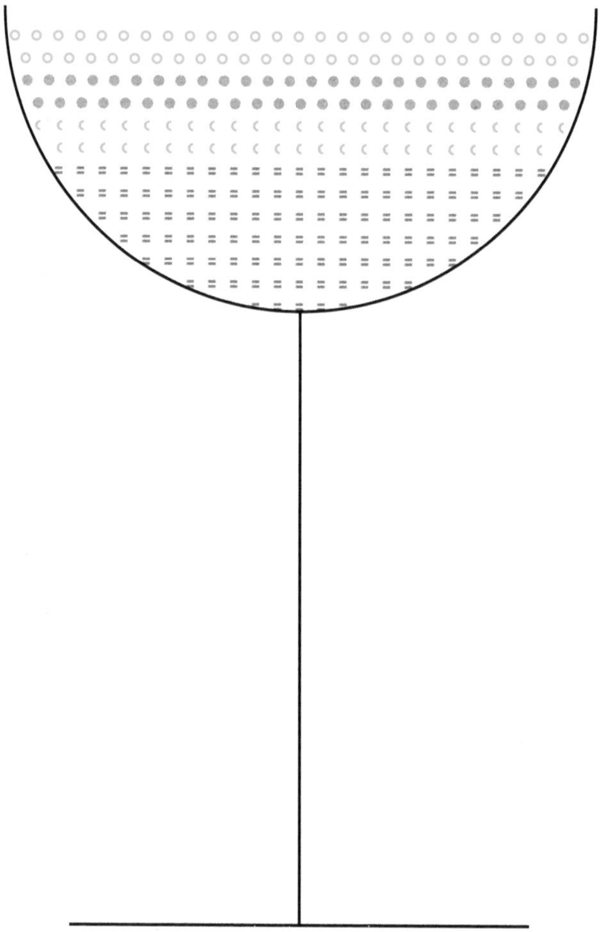

Apple Jack

If the shawl-collar cardigan were a cocktail, it would be this one.
Sasha's Apple Jack was a play on the original cocktail from *The
Savoy Cocktail Book* (from 1930). Much like his favorite sartorial
standby, Sasha adored this drink on a crisp fall evening, but he
also found it a fine choice to hunker down with deep into winter.
Whereas the Savoy's version is simply half an ounce each of Italian
vermouth and Calvados shaken with ice, along with a dash of
Angostura bitters, and strained into a coupe, Sasha's imparts
a finely balanced cornucopia of spices and autumn fruit by way
of apple cider and applejack.

—Georgette Moger-Petraske

½ oz (15 ml) fresh lemon juice
½ oz (15 ml) Simple Syrup (page 20)
½ oz (15 ml) apple cider
1½ oz (45 ml) applejack

Combine the lemon juice, simple syrup, apple cider,
and applejack in a cocktail shaker filled with ice and shake
vigorously until the drink is sufficiently chilled. Strain into
a chilled coupe.

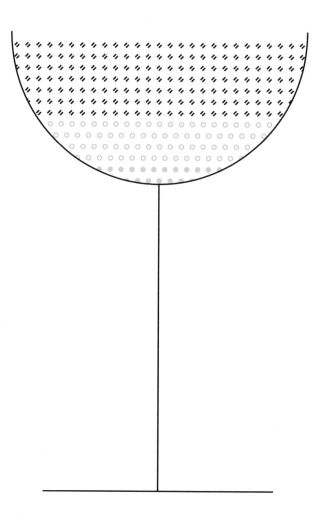

Bee's Knees

One of Sasha's favorite cocktails, this one dates back to the Prohibition era. The addition of lemon juice and honey was once used to mask the taste and smell of bathtub gin.

—Georgette Moger-Petraske

2 oz (60 ml) gin
1 oz (30 ml) fresh lemon juice
¾ oz (22 ml) Honey Syrup (page 21)

Combine the gin, lime juice, and syrup in a cocktail shaker; add 1 large ice cube and shake vigorously until the drink is sufficiently chilled. Strain into a chilled cocktail coupe.

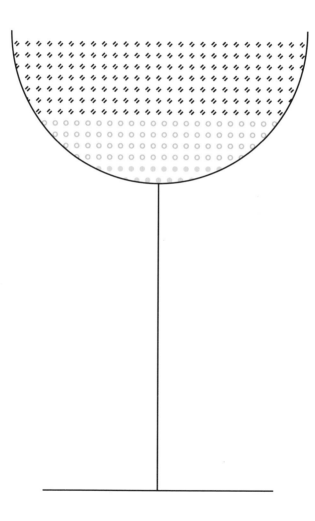

The Business

My favorite Sasha cocktail is The Business. The drink perfectly
embodies Sasha's treasured principle of simplicity and the flip-side
of that principle: his merciless attention to detail. If the drink were
just a tiny bit off, he wouldn't serve it to a dog. When there are only
three ingredients, you have little behind which to hide imper-
fection. The name of the cocktail is a play on words, as it is a slight
variant of the classic Bee's Knees (page 83). Pronounce the names
one after the other, and you'll get it.

—Zachary Gelnaw-Rubin

2 oz (60 ml) gin
1 oz (30 ml) fresh lime juice
¾ oz (22 ml) Honey Syrup (page 21)

Combine the gin, lime juice, and honey syrup in a cocktail
shaker, add 1 large ice cube, and shake vigorously until
the drink is sufficiently chilled. Strain into a chilled coupe.

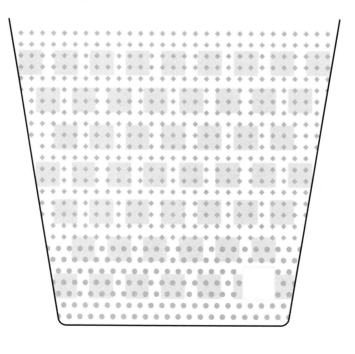

Caipirinha

Sasha loved Caipirinhas and he taught us how to make them properly. With "peasant-style drinks"—those made with muddled citrus and cracked ice—the acidity of the citrus can change drastically from day to day, depending on the size, ripeness, and origin of the fruit. This makes it especially important to taste your first drink of the night, gauge the acidity, and then use that as the benchmark for the rest of the evening. The same also goes for drinks with fresh berries and, basically, any ingredient with the potential for variation.

The other important factor when tasting cracked-ice drinks is coldness and water content. Every facet of your cracked ice is going to affect the amount of water that will melt into the drink as you shake it.

—Karin Stanley

6 lime wedges
2 oz (60 ml) cachaça
¾ oz (22 ml) Simple Syrup (page 20)
1 white sugar cube

Muddle the lime wedges with the cachaça, simple syrup, and sugar cube in a cocktail shaker. Fill with cracked ice and shake vigorously until the drink is sufficiently chilled. Strain into a chilled double rocks glass and add enough cracked ice to fill the glass.

Calvados 75

Sasha was a big fan of sparkling drinks. The Calvados 75 uses Calvados or applejack in lieu of the gin in a classic French 75 (page 161), along with some fresh lemon juice. Topping it off with Champagne or cava brings a certain brunch-like comfort to this cocktail—day or night.

—Lucinda Sterling

1 oz (30 ml) Calvados or applejack
½ oz (15 ml) fresh lemon juice
½ oz (15 ml) Simple Syrup (page 20)
Champagne or cava, for topping off

Combine the Calvados, lemon juice, and simple syrup in a chilled cocktail shaker, add cracked ice, and shake vigorously until the drink is sufficiently chilled. Strain into a Collins glass filled halfway with cracked ice and top off with Champagne or cava.

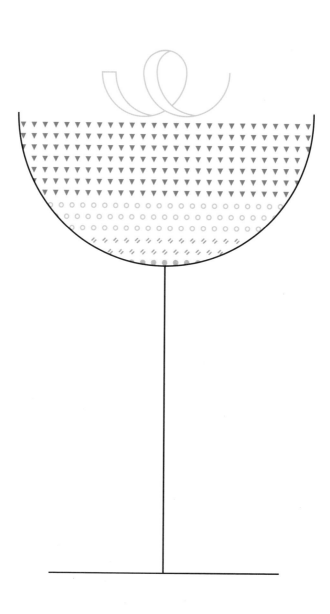

Champs-Élysées

This is a perfect fall cocktail—a riff on the Sidecar, with the orange Curaçao switched out for green Chartreuse, which explodes with complexity. I love a Sidecar; it is simplicity at its finest. But the Champs is wildly unexpected and thought provoking. The first time I had one, I did a cartoon-like double take after the first sip. Most people I served it to did the same.

—Toby Maloney

2 oz (60 ml) Cognac
¾ oz (22 ml) fresh lemon juice
½ oz (15 ml) green Chartreuse
¼ oz (7.5 ml) Simple Syrup (page 20)
A lemon twist, for garnish

Combine the Cognac, lemon juice, Chartreuse, and simple syrup in a cocktail shaker, fill with ice, and shake vigorously until the drink is sufficiently chilled. Strain into a chilled coupe and garnish with the lemon twist.

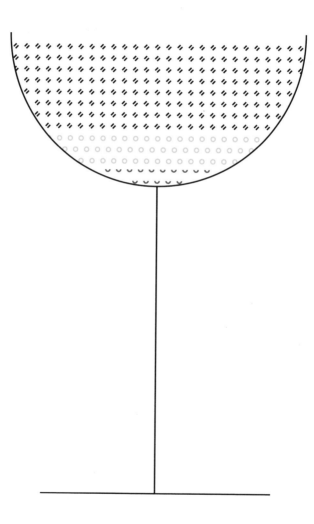

Cosmonaut

This is one of Sasha's cocktails that didn't get as much play as it should have, for some reason—it's excellent. Sasha named it as a jab towards the popularity of the Cosmopolitan, which this drink, emphatically, is not. Much like the Marmalade Cocktail of the 1930s (from Harry Craddock's *The Savoy Cocktail Book*), but a bit sweeter with the use of raspberry preserves rather than orange marmalade, this makes a great aperitif. Sasha's jam brand of choice was Bonne Maman—the jars with the red-and-white-checkered lids.

—Michael Madrusan

2 oz (60 ml) gin
¾ oz (22 ml) fresh lemon juice
1 heaping bar spoon raspberry preserves

Combine the gin, lemon juice, and preserves in a chilled cocktail shaker, fill with ice, and shake vigorously until the drink is sufficiently chilled. Strain into a chilled coupe.

The Sour

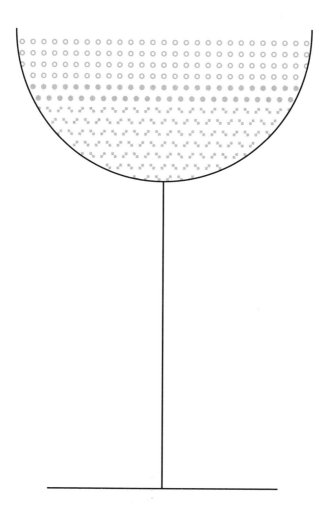

Daiquiri

A perfect Daiquiri is a window into the technique and talent needed to make any shaken drink. For this reason, it is the test drink for anyone who wants to see what a bar or a bartender is all about. Sasha often made his Daiquiris with ⅞ ounce (26 ml) of lime juice because, depending on the lime, a full ounce of juice could make a drink a little too tart. That moment really drove home the importance of tasting every drink—especially the first drinks of the night—because even if you make the drink "right," the ingredients, even in the simplest of drinks, will not always guarantee the same results.

Sasha's pursuit of quality was relentless. If there was a problem with one of the drinks in a round, the whole round would be thrown out and begun again. Every drink had be perfect and they all had to go out together. What mattered always was quietly and unobtrusively doing our part—not for applause or personal gain, but simply because it was the right way to do things.

—Abraham Hawkins

⅞ oz (26 ml) to 1 oz (30 ml) fresh lime juice, to taste
¾ oz (22 ml) Simple Syrup (page 20)
2 oz (60 ml) white rum

Combine the lime juice, simple syrup, and rum in a cocktail shaker, add a 2-inch (5 cm) ice cube, and shake vigorously until the drink is sufficiently chilled. Strain into a chilled coupe.

The Sour

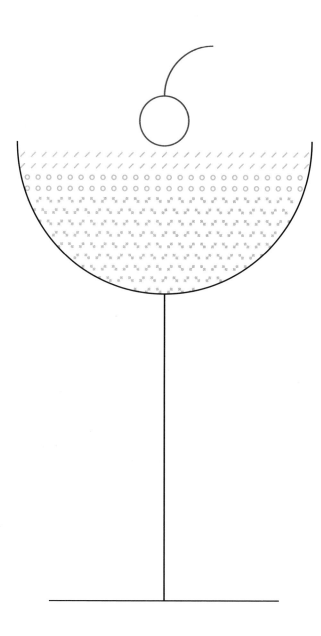

Daiquiri No. 4

Sasha taught me how to make the Daiquiri early on, and he often requested one from me when I was behind the bar at Milk & Honey and at Little Branch. This is yet another drink that demonstrates the elegance that defined Sasha's personal drink style: three ingredients, perfect balance, no fuss.

—Richard Boccato

¾ oz (22 ml) Maraschino liqueur, preferably Luxardo
¾ oz (22 ml) fresh lime juice
2 oz (60 ml) white rum
A Maraschino cherry, for garnish, preferably Luxardo

Combine the Maraschino liqueur, lime juice, and rum in a cocktail shaker filled with ice and shake vigorously until the drink is sufficiently chilled. Strain into a chilled coupe. Garnish with the cherry.

The Sour

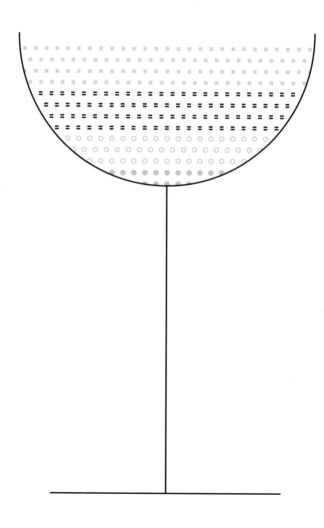

Debbie, Don't

One night when I was working at Dutch Kills, Sasha came in
for some pisco sours. I took the opportunity to have him try out
a funny little cocktail I had been working on. He surprised me
by telling me it was the best drink I had ever come up with.
"If you don't understand why," he told me, "that's OK." I decided to
call it Debbie, Don't after the ghost that haunts the bathrooms at
Dutch Kills.

—Zachary Gelnaw-Rubin

1 oz (30 ml) tequila reposado
1 oz (30 ml) Amaro Averna
¾ oz (22 ml) fresh lemon juice
½ oz (15 ml) maple syrup

Combine the tequila, amaro, lemon juice, and maple syrup in a
cocktail shaker, fill with ice, and shake vigorously until the drink
is sufficiently chilled. Strain into a chilled coupe.

The Sour

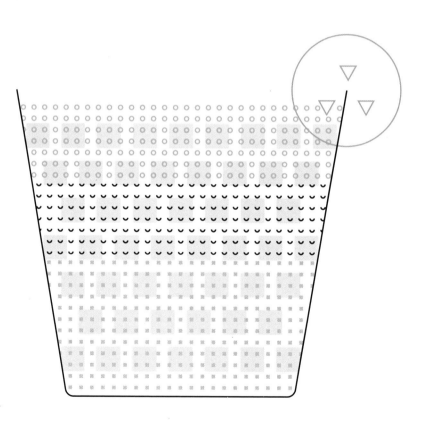

Fresca Platino

Sasha came to the opening of our Dallas bar, Midnight Rambler, in 2014 and worked with us for a day in our lab trying to get to the bottom of several questions of interest to him. One of the things we worked on was trying to nail down a perfect ratio of "acid to sugar," as he had been questioning the usual ratio of 1 oz (30 ml) of lime juice to ¾ oz (22 ml) of simple syrup, thinking that it was no longer correct and that it needed to evolve. Such a ratio was not determined, but this speaks to his focus on the minutiae—never resting, always looking to improve—that made his cocktails extraordinary.

—Chad Solomon & Christy Pope

3 or 4 thin cucumber slices
2 fresh mint sprigs
¾ oz (22 ml) fresh lime juice
¾ oz (22 ml) Mineral Saline (page 23)
2 oz (60 ml) tequila blanco, preferably Tapatio

Reserve 1 cucumber slice for garnish and put the remaining slices and the mint in a cocktail shaker. Add the lime juice and saline and muddle gently. Add the tequila and shake vigorously until the drink is sufficiently chilled. Strain into a rocks glass filled with ice and garnish with the reserved cucumber slice.

The Sour

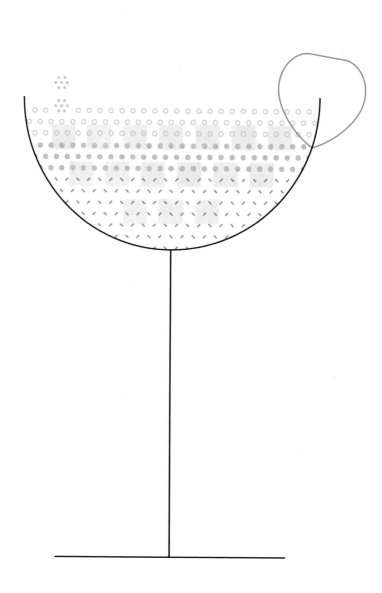

Gabriella

For a cocktail that that would go on the spring and summer menu at The John Dory Oyster Bar, I knew I wanted to use pisco and strawberries. Sasha thought we were onto something tasty, so he had me work on the drink until we decided the strawberry was adding just enough tartness to the drink to scant-measure the lemon. We decided to serve it in a rocks glass with crushed ice and add a pinch of salt on top, mimicking a Gordon's Cup (page 111). The drink was straightforward to make and a real crowd-pleaser.

Sasha also taught me that when you name a cocktail, you do it either after its parent— like the Hemingway Daiquiri, for example—or for something that has a story. I went with the latter method for the Gabriella, after the first Miss Universe from Peru, one of the ancestral homes of pisco.

—Ben Long

1 large strawberry, halved
Scant ¾ oz (22 ml) fresh lemon juice
¾ oz (22 ml) Simple Syrup (page 20)
2 oz (60 ml) pisco
A pinch of kosher salt

Hull one half of the strawberry, combine it with the lemon juice in a cocktail shaker, and muddle gently. Add the simple syrup, pisco, and 1 large ice cube and shake vigorously until the drink is sufficiently chilled. Strain into a rocks glass and add crushed ice until a "high and dry" mountain is formed. Garnish with the remaining strawberry half and the pinch of salt.

The Sour

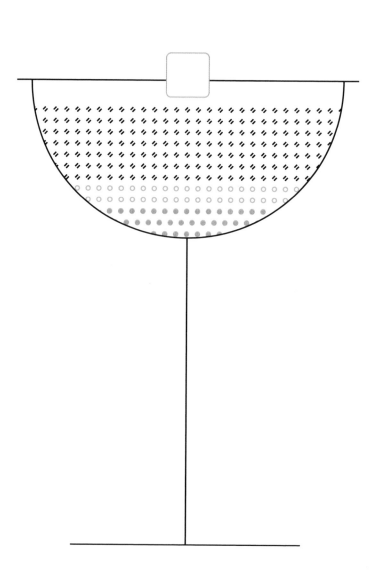

Ginger Cocktail

I can't remember exactly when I met Sasha, because I was
probably only eight years old, or maybe younger. I do recall one
of his visits to my parents' apartment, for a dinner where most
of the Milk & Honey family was present. I loved working at Milk
& Honey. I was just a porter and then a barback, but knowing
I had a bigger family there made me happy.

—Carolyn Gil

2 oz (60 ml) gin
½ oz (15 ml) fresh lime juice
¾ oz (22 ml) Ginger Syrup (page 21)
A piece of candied ginger, for garnish

Combine the gin, lime juice, and ginger syrup in a cocktail
shaker, add 1 large ice cube, and shake vigorously until the
drink is sufficiently chilled. Strain into a chilled coupe and
garnish with the candied ginger.

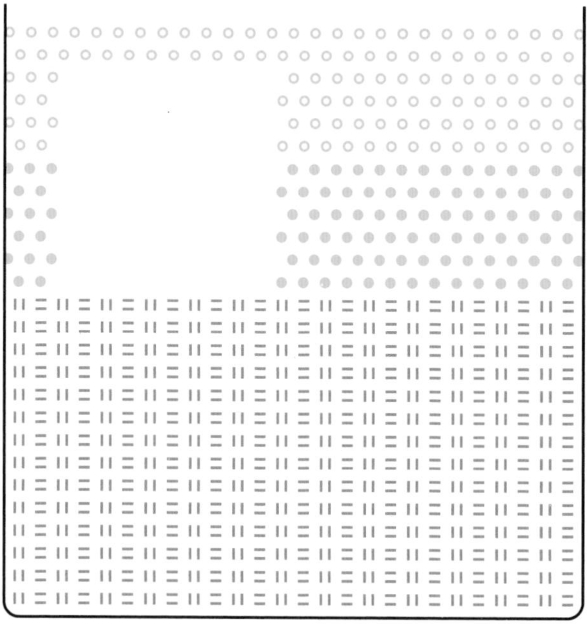

The Gold Rush

The Gold Rush was created by T. J. Siegal, who was Sasha
Petraske's best friend from childhood. T. J. contributed much of
his life savings to help Sasha open Milk & Honey. His knowledge,
wisdom, and advice from his years of experience in the service
industry were bestowed upon me and my colleagues by Sasha as
gospel. The Gold Rush is one of the fundamental examples of
the Milk & Honey cocktail program: three ingredients, perfect
balance, and no fuss.

This drink became a standard in bars the world over, and it
was also the inspiration for The Penicillin (page 127), along with
several other lesser-known variations. Here is the recipe as Sasha
taught it to me.

—Richard Boccato

¾ oz (22 ml) fresh lemon juice
¾ oz (22 ml) Honey Syrup (page 21)
2 oz (60 ml) bourbon

Combine the lemon juice, honey syrup, and bourbon in
a cocktail shaker filled with ice, and shake vigorously until
the drink is sufficiently chilled. Strain into a chilled double
Old Fashioned glass filled with a single large ice cube.

The Sour

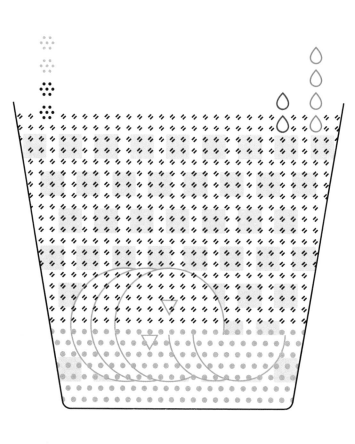

Gordon's Breakfast

We never really told Sasha how much he meant (and still means) to us, but I'm sure he knew. He introduced me to the biggest and most amazing family I'll ever have: Uncle Sammy, Uncle Mickey, and Tío Richie, among others. There's no way for me to thank him enough for that—all the knowledge and the great memories he was part of. This is a variation on one of his signature cocktails, Gordon's Cup (page 111)—it makes a terrific brunch drink.

—Carolyn Gil

2 oz (60 ml) dry London gin
6 lime wedges
¾ oz (22 ml) Simple Syrup (page 20)
3 thin cucumber slices
4 dashes of Cholula hot sauce
2 dashes of Worcestershire sauce,
A pinch of kosher salt
A pinch of freshly ground black pepper

Combine all ingredients in a cocktail shaker. Add 1 cup (240 ml) cracked ice and shake vigorously until the drink sufficiently chilled. Pour into a chilled rocks glass. Finish with a pinch each of salt and freshly ground pepper.

The Sour

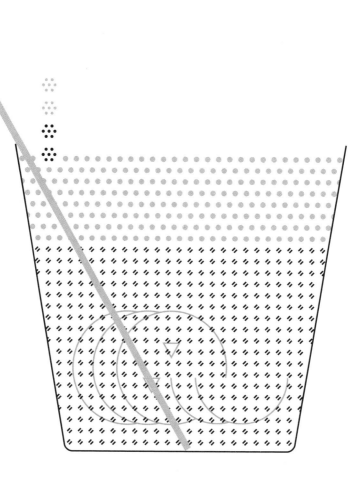

Gordon's Cup

Sasha was definitively known for reviving a lost culture. While he brought back an era of cocktail creation that could not possibly be reinvented without some overlap of the past and present, his intention was to reintroduce classic cocktails made with the best contemporary ingredients. A true Sasha original, this cocktail can be a morning kickstarter, a hangover remedy, or a refreshing nightcap. Cucumber, lime, sugar, and salt cover all the bases.

—Lucinda Sterling

1 small lime, cut into 8 wedges
3 or 4 cucumber slices
¾ oz (22 ml) Simple Syrup (page 20)
2 oz (60 ml) gin
A sprinkling of kosher salt
A sprinkling of freshly cracked black pepper

Combine the lime wedges, cucumber, simple syrup, and gin in a cocktail shaker and muddle to extract the juice from the lime without pulverizing the fruit. Fill the shaker with ice and give it 5 to 6 good shakes. Open the shaker and pour its contents back and forth, separating the lime and cucumber slices from the ice and cocktail; pour the lime and cucumber into a frozen rocks glass, then top off with the ice and liquid. (The muddled lime and cucumber should be at the bottom of the glass; if need be, push the solids to the bottom.) Add a cocktail straw and a sprinkling of salt and pepper.

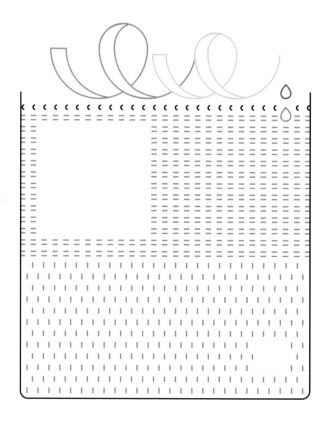

Harvest Sour

Once, Sasha came to the bar and ordered a Harvest Old Fashioned, a widely known drink from the Petraske bar lexicon. It was the first time I had ever heard of the drink, but I knew right away how to make it: an Old Fashioned variation with the spirit body of a Harvest Sour.

It made plain the fact that it isn't important to be constantly innovative—creativity should always take precedence. Sasha's system was a skeleton of a body of drinks—the ratios of the elements are given for the different drink styles, but the elements themselves are infinitely variable. Thinking in these terms exponentially increases one's potential drink repertoire.

—Abraham Hawkins

1 white sugar cube
A dash of Angostura bitters
A dash of Peychaud's bitters
A dash of club soda
1 oz (30 ml) Laird's applejack
1 oz (30 ml) rye whiskey
A lemon twist, for garnish
An orange twist, for garnish

Put the sugar cube in an Old Fashioned glass and soak with both bitters. Add club soda and muddle until a paste forms. Add the brandy and whiskey. Add 1 rock of ice that fits in the bottom of a 6-oz (180 ml) Irish coffee glass. (The ice should not protrude over the lip of the glass.) Stir the drink slowly 9 times or so to lightly chill. Finish with the lemon and orange twists.

The Sour

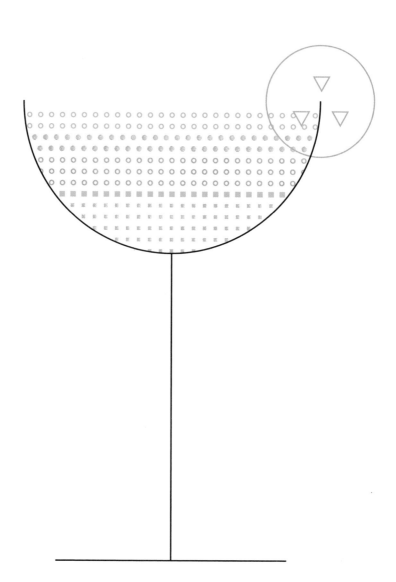

Hole in the Cup

I remember once passing by the service bar when Sasha was correcting a staff member, reminding him to make sure there was less detritus on the surface of the drink in question. I don't think I had heard anyone use the word "detritus" so casually before. I repeat the phrase to myself sometimes, a reminder that gives me a little laugh, especially when I make Sasha's Gordon's Cup (page 111). After attempting to make an absinthe riff on that drink, I came up with something a little off the map that became a real crowd-pleaser, one that disappears as quickly as its name implies.

—Lauren McLaughlin

½ oz (15 ml) fresh lime juice
¾ oz (22 ml) Simple Syrup (page 20)
1 oz (30 ml) fresh pineapple juice
¼ oz (7.5 ml) absinthe
1½ oz (45 ml) tequila blanco
3 thin cucumber slices

Combine the lime juice, simple syrup, pineapple juice, absinthe, tequila, and 2 cucumber slices in a cocktail shaker. Add 12 large pieces of solid ice and shake vigorously until the drink is sufficiently chilled. Strain into a frosted coupe, pouring from high enough to create a nice, fluffy head. Garnish with the remaining cucumber slice.

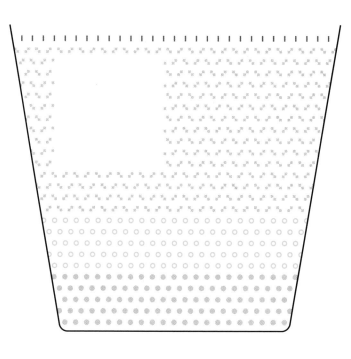

JFK Harris

Over the years, Sasha mentioned a few times that his Holy Grail was for one of his bartenders to invent "the next Mojito." I think Sam Ross came pretty close with the Penicillin (page 127), but I took a couple cracks at it too. One of them was this early effort from my Dutch Kills days.

 This cocktail is a great way to use some red wine that has been open for a day and is on its way out. Float it on top of the cocktail and stir it into the drink for a refreshing summer beverage. I named this drink after the unknown poet Julian Frederick Knipp Harris, a great friend who used to concoct a mint lemonade with red wine for brunch (he also happens to be the same colleague who convinced me to go to Little Branch).

—Zachary Gelnaw-Rubin

2 oz (60 ml) white rum
¾ oz (22 ml) fresh lemon juice
¾ oz (22 ml) Simple Syrup (page 20)
10 to 12 fresh mint leaves
A splash of red wine

Combine the rum, lemon juice, simple syrup, and mint in a cocktail shaker, fill with ice, and shake vigorously until the drink is sufficiently chilled. Strain into a double rocks glass filled with a single large ice cube. Slowly float a finger of red wine on top.

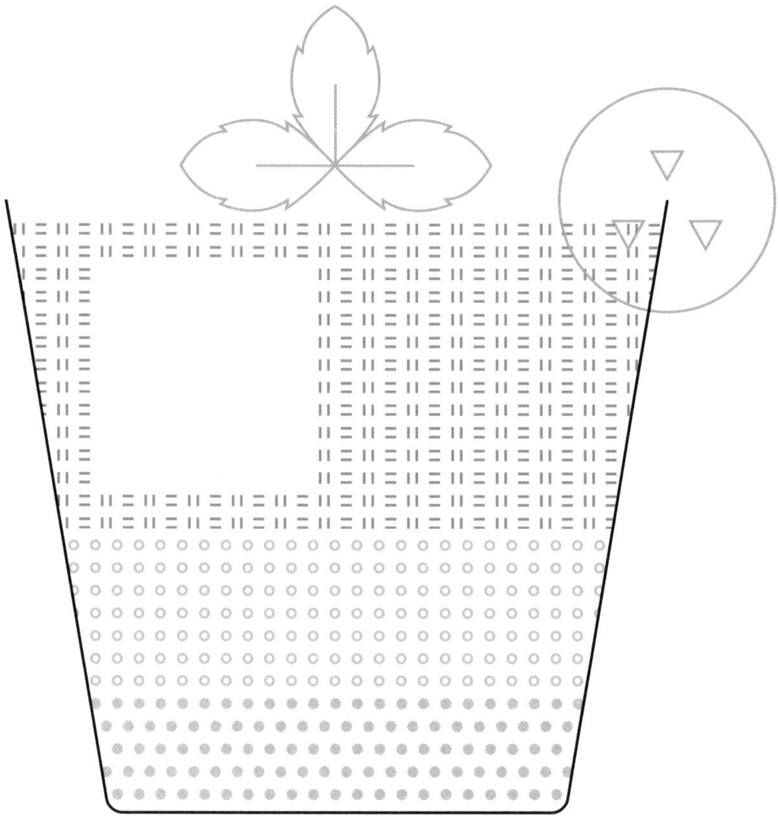

Kentucky Maid

This drink is part of the "Maid" category that was first created for drink maven Lynette Marrero during her tenure at East Side Company, Sasha's first New York City offshoot of Milk & Honey. The first one was done with gin and called the Ol' Biddy, but Sasha disapproved of the name, so we switched to the London Maid. The same drink can be made with any base spirit; just change the first part of the name to align with the origins of the spirit used—in this case, bourbon.

—Sam Ross

2 oz (60 ml) bourbon
1 oz (30 ml) fresh lime juice
¾ oz (22 ml) Simple Syrup (page 20)
8 fresh mint leaves, plus a whole sprig for garnish
3 thin cucumber slices

Combine the bourbon, lime juice, simple syrup, mint leaves, and 2 cucumber slices in a chilled cocktail shaker. Fill the shaker with ice and shake vigorously until the drink is sufficiently chilled. Strain into a chilled rocks glass and garnish with the remaining cucumber slice and the mint sprig.

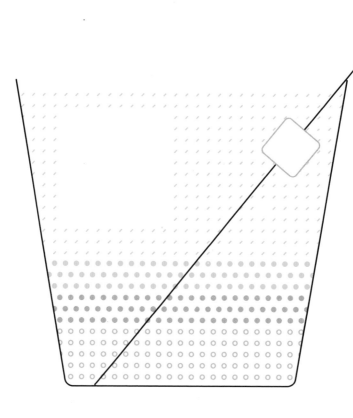

The Medicina Latina

Most of my experiences with Sasha were when he visited Los
Angeles to go over techniques and classics with us at The Varnish.
This was one of the cocktails he taught me. It's a variation on
Sammy's Penicillin (page 127), but it would not be possible
without the signature Milk & Honey Honey Syrup (page 21) and
high-powered Ginger Syrup (page 21). This cocktail should be
shaken and strained over a big rock, but the key is to layer the
mezcal on top, so as to be able to smell the smoke before imbibing it.

—Marcos Tello

2 oz (60 ml) tequila blanco
⅜ oz (11 ml) Honey Syrup (page 21)
½ oz (11 ml) Ginger Syrup (page 21)
¾ oz (22 ml) fresh lime juice
A piece of candied ginger, for garnish
A bar spoon of mezcal

Combine the tequila, honey syrup, ginger syrup, and lime juice
in an ice-filled cocktail shaker and shake vigorously until the
drink is sufficiently chilled. Strain into a rocks glass filled with
1 large ice cube and garnish with the candied ginger. Carefully
float mezcal on top.

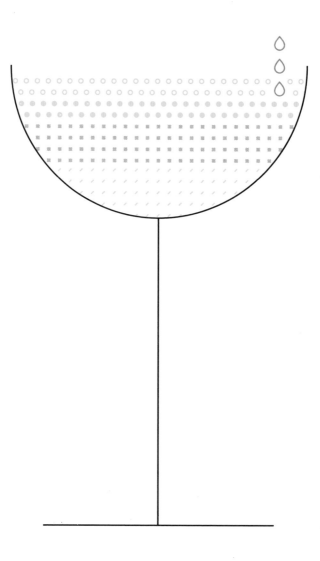

Oaxacanite

After working for a few years at The John Dory Oyster Bar, where Sasha was consulting, I started to feel more confident in creating drinks using Sasha's methods. I was experimenting with mezcal for a spring/summer cocktail menu when Sasha said he didn't like mezcal. He thought its flavor was too dominant in drinks. Naturally I tried even harder to come up with a mezcal drink he would put on the list. The resulting drink was complex and balanced, and when I put one in front of Sasha, he loved it, and immediately passed it for the list. It's named for Oaxaca, the Mexican state that produces mezcal, and it's still my favorite of my own drinks.

—Ben Long

¾ oz (22 ml) fresh lime juice
¾ oz (22 ml) Honey Syrup (page 21)
1 oz (30 ml) tequila blanco
1 oz (30 ml) mezcal, preferably Del Maguey Vida
Scant ½ teaspoon Angostura bitters
A 2-inch (5 cm) grapefruit twist

Combine the lime juice, honey syrup, tequila, mezcal, bitters, and a grapefruit twist in a cocktail shaker and shake vigorously until the drink is sufficiently chilled. Strain into a chilled coupe.

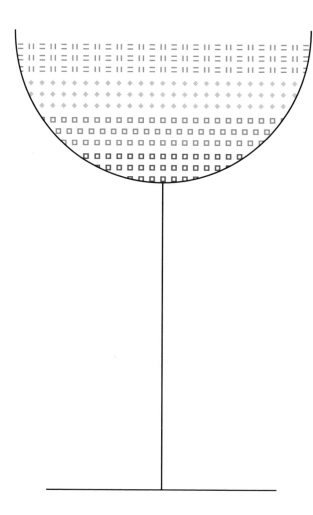

Paper Plane

This cocktail is named after the M.I.A. track that was blasting on repeat the summer we worked on the drink. The song was one of Sasha's guilty pleasures, so far from the 30's jazz we were usually playing at the bar. We created it for another Milk & Honey alum, Toby Maloney, when he was looking for a new cocktail for the summer menu of his Chicago bar, The Violet Hour. It's a riff on the equal-parts brilliance of the Last Word and my favorite amaro. It took a lot of tweaking, but we finally got there.

—Sam Ross

¾ oz (22 ml) bourbon
¾ oz (22 ml) fresh lemon juice
¾ oz (22 ml) Aperol
¾ oz (22 ml) Amaro Nonino

Combine the bourbon, lemon juice, Aperol, and amaro in a chilled cocktail shaker, fill with ice, and shake vigorously until the drink is sufficiently chilled. Strain into a chilled coupe.

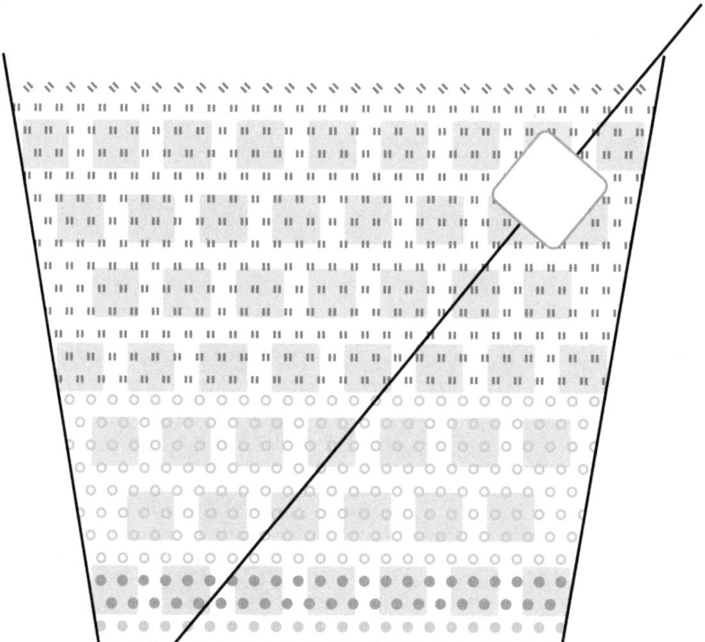

The Penicillin

After we were delivered the recently released line of Compass Box Scotch whiskies, I was playing around with a riff on the Gold Rush (page 107), with the Islay Scotch replacing the bourbon and a little candied ginger thrown in for spice. I then grabbed the super-smoky Peat Monster Scotch and floated some of that on top for nose—it turned out pretty well.

—Sam Ross

2 oz (60 ml) blended Scotch
¾ oz (22 ml) fresh lemon juice
⅜ oz (11 ml) Ginger Syrup (page 21)
⅜ oz (11 ml) Honey Syrup (page 21)
A splash of Islay whisky
A piece of candied ginger, for garnish

Combine the blended Scotch, lemon juice, and both syrups in a cocktail shaker. Fill with ice, and shake vigorously until the drink is sufficiently chilled. Strain into a chilled rocks glass filled with ice. Float the whisky on top and garnish with the candied ginger.

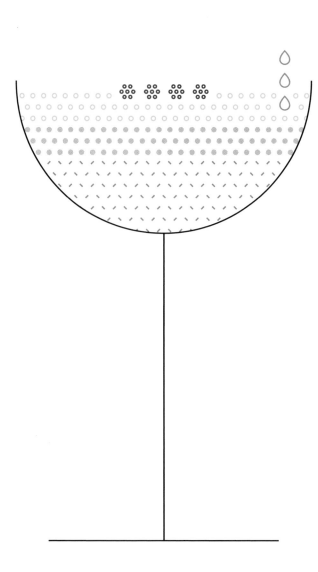

Pisco Sour

"Drink while still frothy." If there is one drink that most reminds me of Sasha, it is this one. When we first opened the Milk & Honey on 23rd Street, he would come in late in the evening to do the a.m. closing shift, and I would switch out and be done for the night. But I would stay to see how the transition went and to soak up as much of Sasha's personality behind the bar as I could. The first thing he would do was make pisco sours for everyone at the bar, his way of greeting new guests and longtime regulars alike.

—Gil Bouhana

¾ oz (22 ml) fresh lemon juice
¾ oz (22 ml) Simple Syrup (page 20)
2 oz (60 ml) pisco
1 egg white from a medium egg
3 dashes Angostura bitters
Freshly grated cinnamon, for garnish

Combine the lemon juice, simple syrup, pisco, and egg white in a cocktail shaker and shake vigorously until the drink is sufficiently chilled. Add a decent amount of ice and shake again for 15 to 20 seconds. Strain into a chilled coupe. Garnish with bitters and a light dusting of cinnamon.

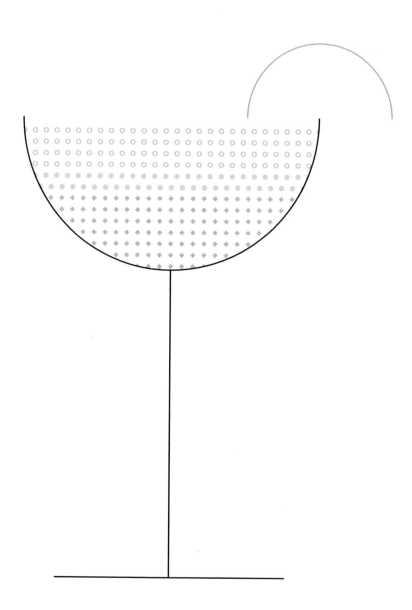

Regal Amburana

This drink sprang from Sasha's relationship with Peter Nevenglosky and Nate Whitehouse from Avua Cachaça. They would frequently visit and sit at a table with Sasha, who would always steer them toward a Bartender's Choice. The Milk & Honey family has always been a fan of Daiquiris, so a variation with Avua Amburana was a perfect fit. I shook the drink with a grapefruit peel acting as a bittering agent instead of bitters—this technique is referred to as a Regal. I sent it out. Sasha came back and said, "That's a drink!" From then on, it was a staple.

—Gil Bouhana

⅞ oz (26 ml) fresh lime juice
¾ oz (22 ml) Honey Syrup (page 21)
2 oz (60 ml) aged cachaça, preferably Avua Amburana
A 2-inch (5 cm) grapefruit twist
A lime wedge, for garnish

Combine the lime juice, honey syrup, cachaça, and grapefruit twist in a cocktail shaker. Fill with ice and shake vigorously until the drink is sufficiently chilled. Strain into a chilled coupe and garnish with the lime wedge.

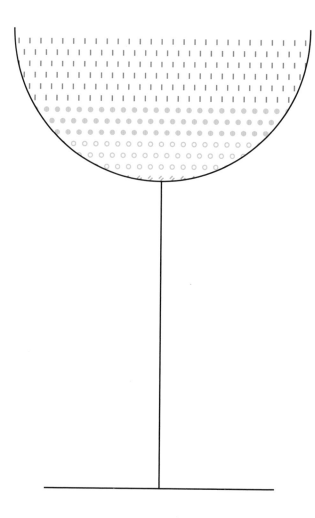

Rye Hummingbird Down

This cocktail goes back to when Sasha, inspired by the Bee's Knees (page 83), swapped lime out for the lemon to create The Business (page 85). Chad Solomon, another mentor/teacher of mine who was Sasha's student, introduced me to the Gin Hummingbird Down and I gave it my own spin with rye. This is a classic "Petraske Family Twist," as we all know that inspiration lies in the smallest variations.

—Marcos Tello

2 oz (60 ml) rye whiskey
¾ oz (22 ml) Honey Syrup (page 21)
¾ oz (22 ml) fresh lemon juice
1 teaspoon green Chartreuse

Combine the whiskey, honey syrup, lemon juice, and Chartreuse in a cocktail shaker, add 1 large ice cube, and shake vigorously until the drink is sufficiently chilled. Strain into a chilled coupe.

The Sour

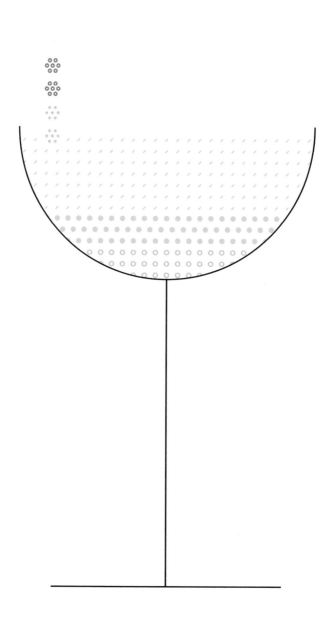

Saladito

This drink is basically a mezcal version of The Business (page 85), with just a bit of cayenne and sea salt on top. It should be shaken with one big rock until the surface of the strained drink almost looks soapy. The froth is part of the textural experience of the drink. It also helps push the salt and cayenne combo forward.

—Marcos Tello

2 oz (60 ml) Espadin mezcal
¾ oz (22 ml) Honey Syrup (page 21)
¾ oz (22 ml) fresh lime juice
A pinch of cayenne pepper
A pinch of fine sea salt

Combine the mezcal, honey syrup, and lime juice in a cocktail shaker, add 1 large ice cube, and shake vigorously until the drink is sufficiently chilled. Strain into a chilled coupe and garnish with a pinch each of cayenne pepper and sea salt.

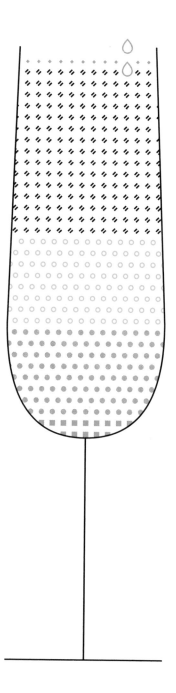

The Seaplane

To create this drink, I thought to myself: If Sasha were my customer, what would I make him? It is a variation of one of his favorite cocktails, the classic French 75 (page 161).

—Joseph Schwartz

1 oz (30 ml) gin
½ oz (15 ml) fresh lemon juice
½ oz (15 ml) Simple Syrup (page 20)
2 dashes orange bitters
Absinthe, for the rinse
Champagne, for topping off

Combine the gin, lemon juice, simple syrup, and bitters in a cocktail shaker filled with ice. Shake vigorously until the drink is sufficiently chilled. Rinse a chilled champagne flute with absinthe and strain the cocktail into the flute. Top off with Champagne.

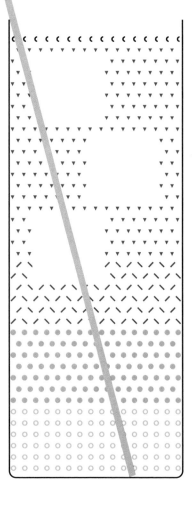

Street & Flynn Special

Traveling to Jamaica with my wife taught me about the geography of Portland Parish, the northeast coast of the island, where her family lives. Among those who lived there at one time were Ian Fleming and Errol Flynn. The latter was a notorious bon vivant, and was often spotted drinking with Sam Street, a Jamaican doctor and hotelier. Their dedication to the good life was so widely known that the parish is sometimes referred to as "The Land of Street and Flynn."

Sasha, like Errol Flynn, had a larger-than-life quality: His style of dress, affinity for nostalgia, the way he rode his bike around town—all that was just Sasha being Sasha. When I first learned of the significance of "The Land of Street and Flynn," I instantly knew the vintage glamour and reputation attached to the reference would appeal to Sasha. This drink combines a Jamaican dark rum with pimento dram, an allspice liqueur popular on the island.

—Joseph Schwartz

1½ oz (45 ml) dark rum, preferably Coruba
½ oz (15 ml) pimento dram
½ oz (15 ml) Ginger Syrup (page 21)
½ oz (15 ml) fresh lime juice
Club soda, for topping off

Combine the rum, dram, ginger syrup, and lime juice in a cocktail shaker and shake vigorously until the drink is sufficiently chilled. Strain into a Collins glass filled with 3 medium ice cubes and top off with club soda. Serve with a straw.

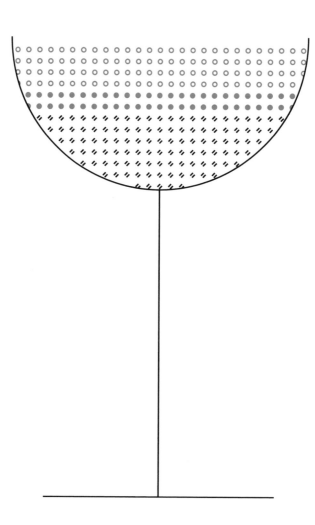

Sugarplum

Sasha always emphasized that a straightforward cocktail was the call of the day. This drink, in keeping with the Milk & Honey ethos of simplicity, was an early creation—a variation on a classic cocktail called The Blinker. Sasha's romantic sense of life was infectious, and he inspired us to be our better selves in ways outside the bars where we worked: on the sidewalk, on the train, in our lives.

When I named the Sugarplum after a pet name given to my wife by her grandmother, he regarded it as a thoughtful element of my courtship duties as a gentleman. Of course he was right. We do better when we take his example and consider bygone or fading customs. Sasha demonstrated the value of those that foster anticipation over gratification, care and quality before convenience, and fairness and generosity governing ambition. For a variation on this cocktail, swap out the gin with tequila.

—Joseph Schwartz

1 oz (30 ml) fresh grapefruit juice
½ oz (15 ml) grenadine syrup
2 oz (60 ml) gin

Combine the juice, syrup, and gin in a cocktail shaker, fill with ice, and shake vigorously until the drink is sufficiently chilled. Strain into a chilled coupe.

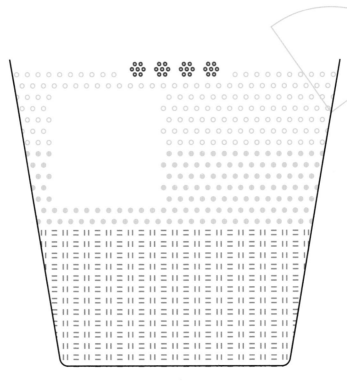

Sutter's Mill

This drink is a variation on one of my favorite cocktails, the Gold Rush (page 107). It's such a straightforward drink, with only three components: lemon, honey syrup, and bourbon. I liked the idea of grated cinnamon over pisco sours as an aromatic, so I tried it on the bourbon, and that was it! As for the name: An American history professor was sitting at a table in the bar, and Sasha brought him the then-nameless drink. As soon as the professor heard the ingredients, he exclaimed, "Sutter's Mill"—where the first gold deposits were found in California.

—Gil Bouhana

2 pineapple wedges
¾ oz (22 ml) fresh lemon juice
¾ oz (22 ml) Honey Syrup (page 21)
2 oz (60 ml) bourbon
Freshly grated cinnamon, for garnish

Combine 1 pineapple wedge, the lemon juice, and honey syrup in a cocktail shaker and muddle until the pineapple is broken up. Add the bourbon, fill with ice, and shake vigorously until the drink is sufficiently chilled. Strain into a chilled double rocks glass filled with 1 large ice cube. Garnish with the remaining pineapple wedge and dust with cinnamon.

The Sour

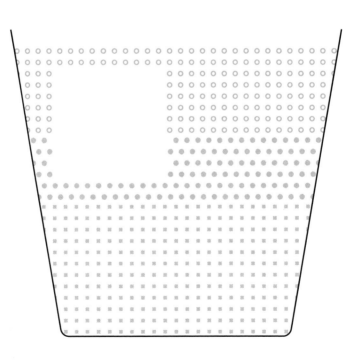

Tequila Eastside

The Eastside was a pivotal drink at Milk & Honey that got people into drinking gin at a time when vodka reigned supreme and gin was still polarizing. This is a drink that made its way into the Milk & Honey lexicon through bartender Chad Solomon. He had worked for a time at another Lower East Side bar called Libation, where George Delgado, a gentleman and barman, had put together the cocktail list and trained the opening staff. Chad had a drink called the Eastside Fizz made with sugar, mint, lime, soda, and Hendrick's Gin—a gin touted for the cucumber in its makeup. We took the idea of his drink and molded it the Milk & Honey way, using tequila as the base. Per Sasha's suggestion, the spirit base was brought down to 1 1/2 oz (45 ml) rather than 2 oz (60 ml), because of the more aggressive nature of the agave spirit.

—Christy Pope

2 or 3 thin cucumber slices
A handful of fresh mint sprigs
1 oz (30 ml) fresh lime juice
¾ oz (22 ml) Simple Syrup (page 20)
1½ oz (45 ml) tequila blanco, preferably El Jimador

Put the cucumbers and mint in a cocktail shaker, add the lime juice and simple syrup, and gently muddle. Add the tequila and 1 large ice cube and shake vigorously until the drink is sufficiently chilled. Strain into a chilled rocks glass filled with 1 large ice cube.

The Sour

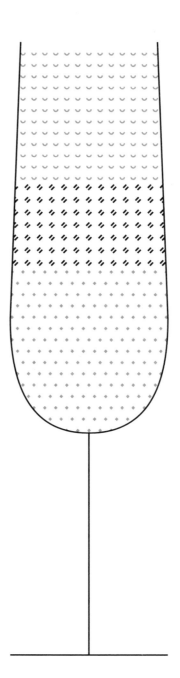

The Tie Binder

Sasha and I returned from our honeymoon on the Belmond Venice-Simplon Orient Express craving the white peach Bellinis that had been served onboard. We learned the technique of making the peach purée after a few trial runs in our kitchen in Hudson, New York, where sweet peaches were in abundance that summer. This cocktail is a variation on the Bellinis we had on the train, with a splash of Monkey 47—our special-occasion gin.

—Georgette Moger-Petraske

1½ oz (45 ml) White Peach Purée (page 24)
1 oz (30 ml) gin, preferably Monkey 47 Schwarzwald
2 oz (60 ml) Champagne if you're feeling fancy,
    prosecco if it's Tuesday

Combine the purée and gin in a champagne flute. Slowly top off with the Champagne, stirring gently to incorporate the pink color and create a foamy top.

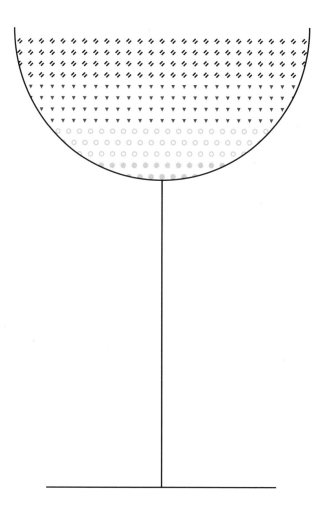

Too Soon?

Sasha once told me that the Cynar logo was one of the most
beautiful he'd ever seen. He had commissioned a regular, in
exchange for free drinks, to stencil and paint it behind the bar at
Milk & Honey, where it's still faintly visible on the exposed brick.
While Sasha considered Cynar the vilest-tasting liqueur—often
joking that in hell you'd ask for a glass of ice water and get served
a glass of hot Cynar—he loved this drink. As the name implies,
it is a pre-dinner aperitif, designed to be light, bitter, and bright.

—Sam Ross

1 oz (30 ml) gin
1 oz (30 ml) Cynar
¾ oz (22 ml) fresh lemon juice
½ oz (15 ml) Simple Syrup (page 20)
2 thin orange slices

Combine the gin, Cynar, lemon juice, simple syrup, and orange
slices in a cocktail shaker, fill with ice, and shake vigorously
until the drink is sufficiently chilled. Strain into a chilled coupe.

The Sour

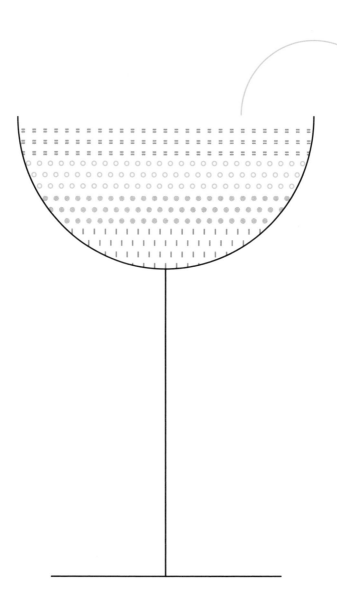

Turnpike

Another early Milk & Honey take on the sour, this was created to feature Laird's applejack and rye. The name refers to the highway that links New Jersey, home of Laird's, and Pennsylvania, home to Monongahela rye whiskey—to New York.

—Joseph Schwartz

¾ oz (22 ml) applejack
¾ oz (22 ml) fresh lemon juice
¾ oz (22 ml) Simple Syrup (page 20)
1 oz (30 ml) rye whiskey, preferably Monongahela
A lemon wedge, for garnish

Combine the applejack, lemon juice, simple syrup, and whiskey in a cocktail shaker and fill with ice. Shake vigorously until the drink is sufficiently chilled, then strain into a chilled coupe. Garnish with the lemon wedge.

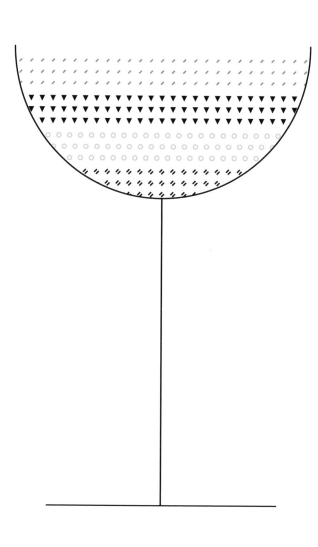

Water Lily

I recall an evening in 2007, when Georgette was elegantly poised
at the bar with a twinkle of curiosity in her eye and nary a beverage
in sight. She asked me to make her something containing violet
syrup and gin. I don't recall much fussing with the specs after the
first few attempts, as Georgette's palate—and her understanding
of spirits and cocktails—rival those of the most seasoned veterans
within the Petraske family of bartenders.

When prompted for a name for the cocktail, we somehow
arrived at her middle name—Lillian. "Water Lily" seemed like
a good fit, since the drink has a crisp yet ethereal aspect.

—Richard Boccato

¾ oz (22 ml) orange liqueur, such as Cointreau
¾ oz (22 ml) Violette Syrup (page 20)
¾ oz (22 ml) fresh lemon juice
¾ oz (22 ml) gin
A lemon twist, for garnish

Combine the orange liqueur, violette syrup, lemon juice,
and gin in a cocktail shaker filled with ice. Shake vigorously
until the drink is sufficiently chilled, and strain into a coupe.
Twist the lemon peel over the glass to extract the oils, then
discard the twist.

The Sour

The Highball

Served Long, Including Traditional Fizzes

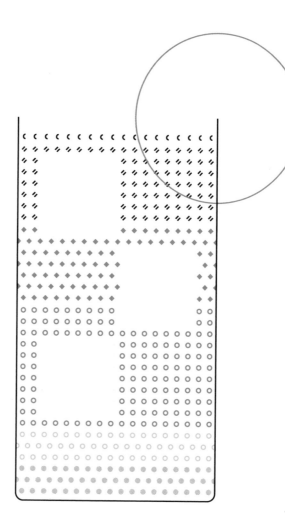

Bicycle Thief

Not long after I became a regular fixture at Little Branch I met
Sasha. Everything about him, including his attire, was in complete
order, from hatless head to wingtips. Once he said to me, "May
I make a sartorial suggestion? Unbutton the bottom button of your
coat." And thus I learned the first of many lessons on manhood
from Sasha: the "sometimes, always, never" rules of men's fashion.

Setting aside his colossal achievements in the realm of
cocktails and dress code, Sasha's greatest contribution was his
decency—not just in service and hospitality, but in human conduct
in general.

This drink is a collaboration with my once Dutch Kills
colleague, Abraham Hawkins, and named the Bicycle Thief for
the iconic Italian film. A delicious variation on this is my Tarzan
Cocktail. Just swap out the grapefruit juice for fresh pineapple juice.

—Zachary Gelnaw-Rubin

1 oz (30 ml) gin
1 oz (30 ml) Campari
1½ oz (45 ml) fresh grapefruit juice
½ oz (15 ml) fresh lemon juice
½ oz (15 ml) Simple Syrup (page 20)
Club soda, for topping off
A thin orange slice, for garnish

Combine the gin, Campari, grapefruit juice, lemon juice, and
simple syrup in a highball glass filled with a long Collins cube
or 3 medium ice cubes. Top off with soda and garnish with the
orange slice.

Bottlerocket

I worked at Milk & Honey until we moved from Eldridge Street
to 23rd Street, where Sasha made me the head bartender. It was
a job that was made easy by the most brilliant staff anyone could
have put together.

In a lot of ways, this drink has to be made to taste: Jalapeños
range in heat, as do people's levels of tolerance for heat. This
cocktail has a really pretty head, thanks to the honey in the drink,
which will froth nicely. It is roughly the same color as The Business
(page 111), another of Sasha's drinks, though the club soda makes it
slightly paler.

—Theo Lieberman

2 oz (60 ml) tequila blanco
¾ oz (22 ml) fresh lime juice
¾ oz (22 ml) Honey Syrup (page 21)
One ¼-inch (5 mm) thick jalapeño slice
Club soda, for topping off

Combine the tequila, lime juice, honey syrup, and jalapeño in
a cocktail shaker, fill the shaker with ice, and shake vigorously
until the drink is sufficiently chilled. Strain into a Collins glass
filled with ice and top off with the club soda.

The Highball

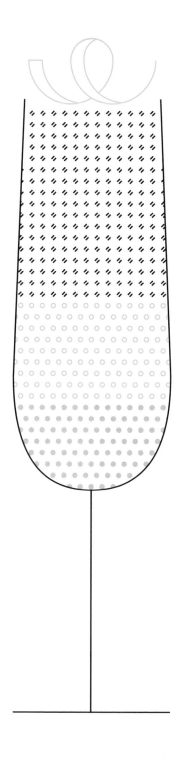

French 75

This is a classic, and one of Sasha's all-time favorite cocktails—
simple, elegant, and celebratory. In the Milk & Honey fashion,
the house recipe imparts Cognac, while *The Savoy Cocktail Book*
calls for gin. Both variations, in the immortal words of the author
Mr. Harry Craddock, "hit with remarkable precision."

—Georgette Moger-Petraske

1 oz (30 ml) Cognac or gin, if requested
½ oz (15 ml) fresh lemon juice
½ oz (15 ml) Simple Syrup (page 20)
Champagne, prosecco, or cava
A lemon twist, for garnish

Combine the Cognac, lemon juice, and simple syrup in a
cocktail shaker and shake vigorously with a small piece of
cracked ice. Strain into the small half of the shaker and top with
Champagne directly in the shaker. Transfer or "roll" into a
chilled champagne flute or coupe. Garnish with a lemon twist.

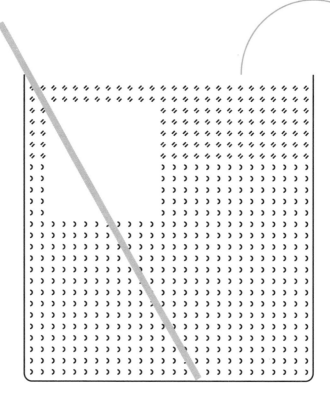

Gin & Tonic

In 2004, I went into a bar on the Lower East Side called Milk & Honey. Although I didn't know Sasha then, it was my first experience with the ethics and values of offhand excellence he insisted upon from himself and his colleagues.

I worked in the Milk & Honey family for several years, and coming from an acting background, my actress girlfriend and I decided that a Los Angeles move was inevitable. Months later, Sasha came to visit. He made us Gin & Tonics, but upon realizing we were out of limes, suddenly left the apartment, returning minutes later with a guayabera full of little green fists of citrus. "I saw that tree a block from your place this morning."

Handing me my drink, Sasha asked, "Eric, do you like making lists?" "I have obsessive-compulsive tendencies so I kinda have to make lists," I replied. "Well, then you'll be fine at opening a bar."

—Eric Alperin

2 oz (60 ml) gin
1 bottle (6-oz/180 ml) tonic water (your favorite)
A lime wedge, for garnish

Pour the gin into a double Old Fashioned glass filled with 1 large ice cube. Serve with the bottle of your favorite tonic on the side. (Sasha and I enjoyed Fever Tree.) A metal straw and lime wedges—preferably from fruit picked off a tree a block from your apartment—make the drink all the more special. Garnish with the lime wedge.

The Highball

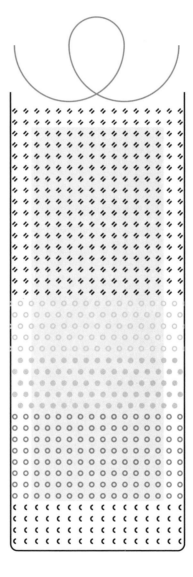

Grapefruit Collins

In the beginning at Milk & Honey, everything Sasha did was a revelation. I was coming from years in clubs and restaurant bars where nothing but speed mattered. The bars in the former were basically holding areas for people waiting to sit down—the drinks were big and strong. While it all might seems obvious now, there were some basic things Sasha did that were game changers. Small things made a huge impact: fresh juices, ice, and club soda from small bottles. He would change just one thing in a cocktail and it would change the way you thought about cocktails as a whole.

—Toby Maloney

2 oz (60 ml) gin
¾ oz (22 ml) fresh lemon juice
¾ oz (22 ml) Simple Syrup (page 20)
1 oz (30 ml) fresh grapefruit juice
½ oz (15 ml) club soda
A grapefruit twist, for garnish

Combine the gin, lemon juice, and simple syrup in a cocktail shaker, fill with ice, and shake vigorously until the drink is sufficiently chilled. Strain into a Collins glass filled with 1 large Collins ice cube and top off with the grapefruit juice and club soda. Garnish with the grapefruit twist.

The Highball

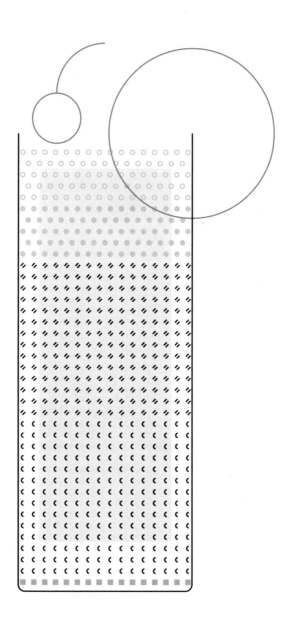

Hayes Fizz

In some ways, there couldn't be a more Milk & Honey drink—
and a more personally influential drink for us—than the Hayes
Fizz. Since the beginning, Milk & Honey was frequented by its
cast of regulars, one of whom was Reed Hayes. Milk & Honey's
uniqueness inspired patrons to bring gifts, or "offerings," to the
bar. Particularly alluring was absinthe, banned at the time in the
States, from trips abroad. Reed liked to add a lil' nip of it to his
Tom Collins, and such was the origin of the Hayes Fizz. Reed was
fond of saying, "Absinthe makes the heart grow fonder."

—Chad Solomon & Christy Pope

¾ oz (22 ml) fresh lemon juice
¾ oz (22 ml) Simple Syrup (page 20)
2 oz (60 ml) gin
2 oz (60 ml) club soda
Absinthe or Pernod, for the rinse
An orange slice, for garnish
A cocktail cherry, for garnish

Combine the lemon juice, simple syrup, and gin in a cocktail
shaker, add 1 large ice cube, and shake vigorously until the drink
is sufficiently chilled. Put a large Collins ice cube in a chilled
Collins glass and rinse with absinthe. Strain the cocktail into the
glass and garnish with the orange slice and cherry.

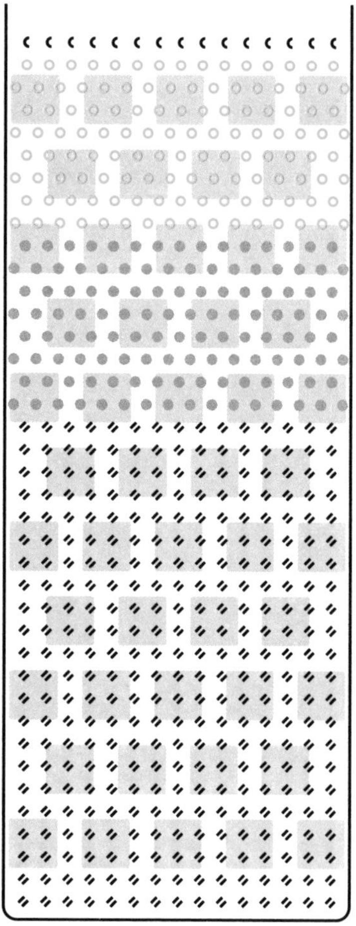

KT Collins

One of Sasha's consulting commissions was for The John Dory Oyster Bar, and he chose to be compensated by a weekly tab of bivalves, crustaceans, and cocktails. We always sat at the same inconspicuous table in the back hall, reading our newspapers, passing an afternoon over East Coast oysters and several KT Collinses, named for one of my favorite ladies in the cocktail industry, Katie Stipe. On occasion, Sasha and I would opt for a Bloom Collins—essentially the same libation muddled with fennel instead of celery, and no salt.

—Georgette Moger-Petraske

2 matchstick-size strips of celery
¾ oz (22 ml) fresh lemon juice
¾ oz (22 ml) Simple Syrup (page 20)
A generous pinch of kosher salt
2 oz (60 ml) gin
Club soda, for topping off

Muddle the celery in a cocktail shaker. Fill the shaker with ice, add the lemon juice, simple syrup, salt, and gin, and shake vigorously until the drink is sufficiently chilled. Strain into a Collins glass filled with ice. Top off with club soda.

The Highball

Palma Fizz

Sasha created this cocktail, one of the few made with vodka at Milk & Honey, for his childhood friend Joanie Ellen. Also known as the Moscow Mule or Vodka Buck, it is traditionally finished with a few drops of rosewater. Nowadays people use an atomizer and spray the rosewater instead, either as a preliminary rinse of the glass or directly on top of the completed cocktail.

—Richard Boccato

½ lime
2 oz (60 ml) vodka
4 to 6 oz (120 to 180 ml) ginger beer
Rosewater, for serving

Squeeze ½ oz (15 ml) of lime juice into a Collins glass (or a Moscow Mule mug) and drop in the empty half lime shell. Add 2 or 3 ice cubes, pour in the vodka, and fill with the ginger beer. Add a few drops of rosewater or spray the rosewater over the cocktail.

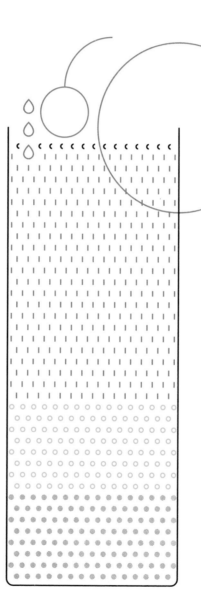

Ross Collins

Sasha met everyone in my family and said, "I can't say anything
bad about any of them, save for your brother Toby—he's too
handsome." The Ross Collins, named for a certain famous cocktail
family from Australia, is a whiskey take on the Tom Collins,
with some body furnished by the orange slices and Angostura.

—Sam Ross

2 oz (60 ml) rye whiskey
¾ oz (22 ml) fresh lemon juice
¾ oz (22 ml) Simple Syrup (page 20)
3 thin range slices
3 dashes Angostura bitters
Club soda, for topping off
A brandied cherry, for garnish

Combine the whiskey, lemon juice, simple syrup, 2 orange
slices, and bitters in a cocktail shaker, fill with ice, and shake
vigorously until the drink is sufficiently chilled. Strain into
a Collins glass, top off with club soda, and garnish with the
remaining orange slice and the brandied cherry.

The Highball

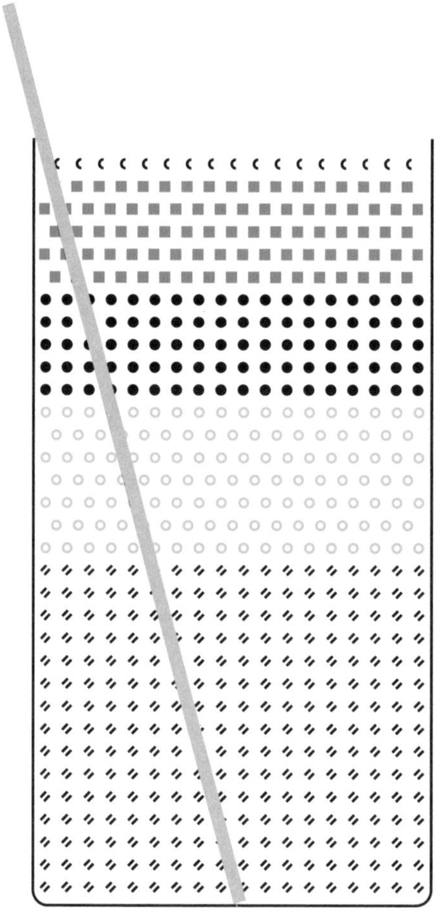

Silver Fox

On the subject of original or signature cocktails, Sasha always reminded me that there were more than enough classics to go around and that a neophyte bartender would do best to learn them inside and out prior to trying his or her hand at conjuring up new and interesting drinks. Basically, know your history before attempting to reinvent the wheel. So this drink essentially remains a Silver Fizz, but with orgeat in place of the simple syrup, and its name reflects that. 'Nuff said.

—Richard Boccato

1 egg white from a medium egg
½ oz (15 ml) Orgeat Syrup (page 22)
¾ oz (22 ml) fresh lemon juice
1½ oz (45 ml) gin
Club soda, for topping off
½ oz (15 ml) amaretto or Faretti Biscotti liqueur

Combine the egg white, orgeat syrup, lemon juice, and gin in a cocktail shaker and shake to emulsify the mixture. Add one large ice cube and shake vigorously until the drink is sufficiently chilled. Strain into a chilled 9-oz (270 ml) highball glass. Top off with soda and float the amaretto or Faretti on top. Serve with a straw.

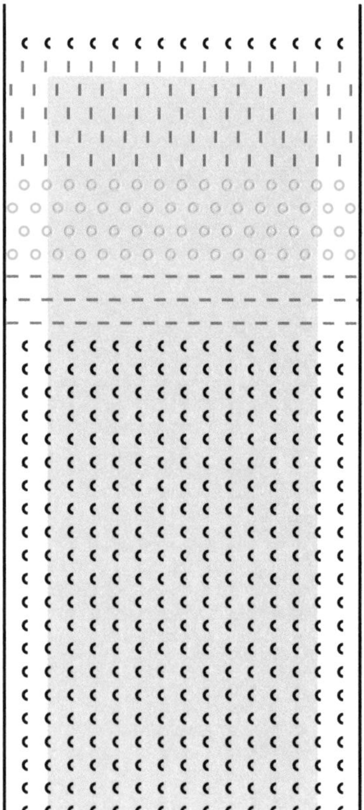

Silver Lining

This drink was one of mine at Milk & Honey circa 2001. Sasha had brought in Licor 43, the Spanish liqueur, and asked that I come up with something. I had been making a lot of Rye Fizzes and Silver Rye Fizzes at the time, when Van Winkle 13 was readily available— and affordable. So this was the result. The name came from one of our regular customers. We were discussing possibilities and I described some of the conventions for using the word "silver" for drinks that included egg white. Coincidentally, Chet Baker was a regular feature of the music played in the bar. I don't know that his song "Look for the Silver Lining" was a direct influence, but I like to think so.

—Joseph Schwartz

1½ oz (45 ml) rye whiskey
1 egg white from a medium egg
¾ oz (22 ml) fresh lemon juice
¾ oz (22 ml) Licor 43 or another citrus blend liqueur
6 oz (180 ml) club soda

Combine the whiskey, egg white, lemon juice, and Licor 43 in a cocktail shaker and shake to emulsify the mixture. Add 1 large ice cube and shake vigorously until the drink is sufficiently chilled. Strain into a chilled Collins glass filled long Collins ice cube. Top off with club soda until the froth reaches the rim of the glass. Let stand for a moment so the foam settles, then add more club soda to raise the froth just over the rim of the glass.

The Highball

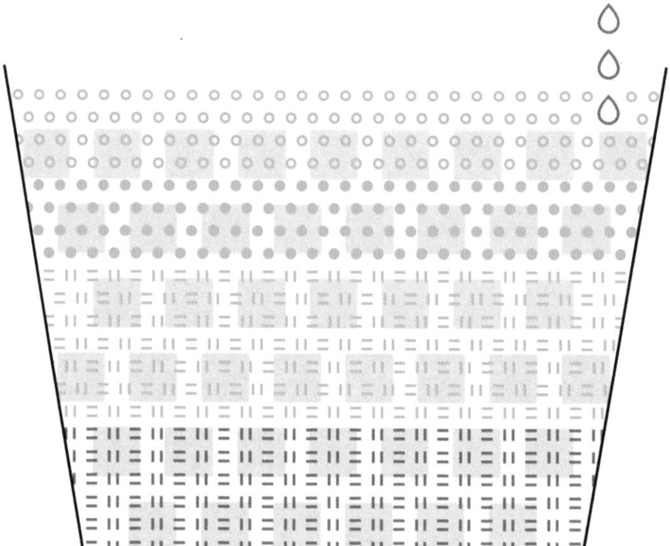

The Stark

This cocktail reminds me of my barback days at Milk & Honey. I was only a teenager and yet I was working in one of the most prestigious bars in New York City. The Stark may be a very simple drink, but the love put into it makes it very special.

—Carolyn Gil

½ oz (15 ml) fresh lemon juice
½ oz (15 ml) Honey Syrup (page 21)
¾ oz (22 ml) yellow Chartreuse
1½ oz (45 ml) Kentucky bourbon
Angostura bitters

Combine the lemon juice, honey syrup, Chartreuse, and bourbon in a cocktail shaker, fill with ice, and shake vigorously until the drink is sufficiently chilled. Strain into a rocks glass and add cracked ice and a generous float of bitters.

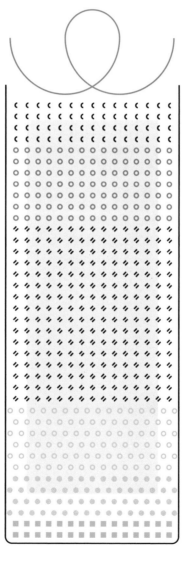

Tritter Collins

Sasha always had a kind word and an immediate reservation for Mr. Tritter, a Milk & Honey regular. Sasha thought him a wonderful guest and an erudite conversationalist, with an inquiring mind. There were not many of those patrons back then. The Tritter Collins is a Grapefruit Collins with a dash of absinthe. It quickly became a drink I made all the time in the summer months.

—Toby Maloney

2 oz (60 ml) gin
¾ oz (22 ml) fresh lemon juice
¾ oz (22 ml) Simple Syrup (page 20)
¼ oz (7.5 ml) absinthe
1 oz (30 ml) fresh grapefruit juice
½ oz (15 ml) club soda
A grapefruit twist, for garnish

Combine the gin, lemon juice, simple syrup, and absinthe in a cocktail shaker, fill with ice, and shake vigorously until the drink is sufficiently chilled. Strain into a Collins glass filled with a long Collins ice cube and top off with the grapefruit juice and club soda. Garnish with the grapefruit twist.

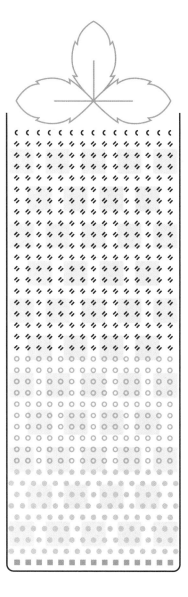

Tritter Rickey

This rickey, created for Mr. Tritter, a Milk & Honey regular, is essentially a Southside Fizz (aka Mint Rickey) with an absinthe rinse.

—Richard Boccato

2 oz (60 ml) gin
1 oz (30 ml) fresh lime juice
¾ oz (22 ml) Simple Syrup (page 20)
Absinthe, for the rinse
Club soda, for topping off
A fresh mint sprig, for garnish

Combine the gin, lime juice, and simple syrup in a cocktail shaker, fill with ice, and shake vigorously until the drink is sufficiently chilled. Coat a Collins glass with and absinth rinse and fill the glass with ice. Strain the drink into the glass, top off with club soda, and garnish with the mint sprig.

The Fix

Cobblers, Swizzles, and Peasant Cocktails

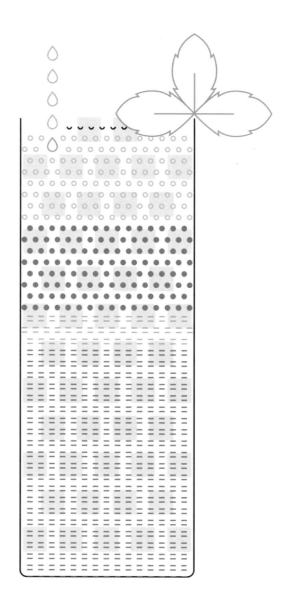

Asbury Park Swizzle

This modern take on the Queen's Park Swizzle (pages 197 and 199), is a nod to New Jersey native Bruce Springsteen, whose debut album was *Greetings from Asbury Park*. Its base spirit is Jersey Lightning, a white applejack from the New Jersey–based Laird & Company. There are also several deviations from the Queen's Park Swizzle template.

The variables that go into making a cocktail—measurement, chill, water content, ice, bubble structure—are what made Sasha a great innovator.

—Chad Solomon & Christy Pope

3 fresh mint sprigs
¾ oz (22 ml) fresh lemon juice
¾ oz (22 ml) Honey Syrup (page 21)
¼ oz (7.5 ml) apple liqueur, preferably Berentzen's
2 oz (60 ml) white applejack, preferably Laird's Jersey Lightning
2 drops Mineral Saline (page 23)
4 to 5 dashes A.P.P. Bitters (page 23)
1 dash House Orange Bitters (page 24)

Combine 2 mint sprigs, lemon juice, honey syrup, and apple liqueur in a cocktail shaker and gently muddle. Add the applejack and mineral saline, then swirl to incorporate. Pour the cocktail into a Collins glass and add crushed ice to come just under the rim of the glass. Add both bitters and lightly swizzle the drops into a red layer on top of the ice. Top with more ice, shaping it into a cone, and garnish with the remaining mint sprig.

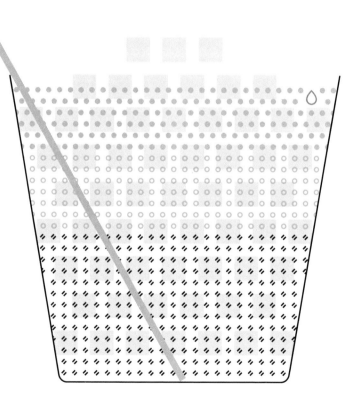

Bin & Gitters

The first time Sasha ordered a Bin & Gitters from me, I thought I misheard him—it was a funny name after all. I asked my colleagues—none of us knew it. Was I really going to have to admit to my boss that I didn't know how to make his drink? But then I realized Sasha wouldn't care if I didn't know the drink—he'd relish teaching me.

"It's a gimlet on crushed ice with a bitters float," Sasha said. I instantly knew it meant a lime drink using a one-to-three-quarters sour-to-sweet ratio. The fact that Sasha didn't specify the base spirit or the bitters meant the defaults were gin and Angostura. I placed the drink on the tray and remembered another Sasha truism: "No garnish for a bartender."

—Karin Stanley

¾ oz (22 ml) Simple Syrup (page 20)
1 oz (30 ml) fresh lime juice
2 oz (60 ml) gin
A dash of Angostura bitters
A lime wedge, for garnish

Combine the simple syrup, lime juice, and gin in a cocktail shaker and shake to mix. Pour into a chilled double rocks glass. Add crushed ice to come three-quarters of the way up the sides of the glass, then add bitters to create a discernable layer of coloration. Top with more crushed ice, shaping it into a cone. Serve with a straw.

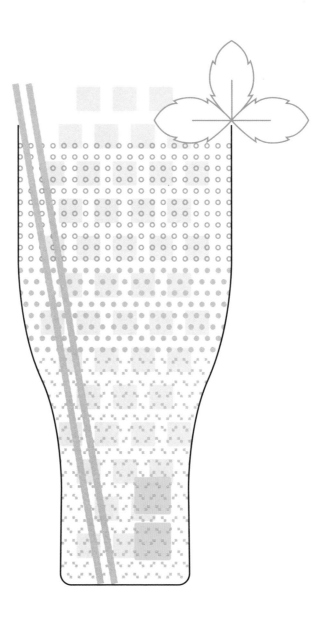

Eskimo's Kiss

Sasha's drink of choice seemed to be a Mojito (page 195), and often he would get what he called an "Eskimo's Kiss," which was essentially a double Mojito in a large glass with two straws, though I can't recall ever seeing him share one. He always used one straw to taste, took the second straw out, and brought it to one of the clerks at Kinko's down the street, where he would barter the cocktail for printing services.

Like the Petraske Mojito, the Eskimo's Kiss is as perfect, simple, and straightforward as could be—a shining example of Sasha's interpretation of the classics. Just fresh ingredients on crushed ice, no soda. The mint at the bottom of the glass adds flavor to the melting ice. The sugar cubes likewise enrich the drink's flavor as it is thinned by melting ice.

—Abraham Hawkins

10 to 12 fresh mint leaves, plus whole sprigs for garnish
2 Demerara sugar cubes (or 1 if it is giant)
2 oz (60 ml) fresh lime juice
1½ oz (45 ml) Simple Syrup (page 20)
4 oz (120 ml) white rum

Combine the mint leaves and sugar cubes in a cocktail shaker and soak the sugar in the lime juice and simple syrup. Then muddle gently—ideally crushing the sugar into a paste, without more than lightly bruising the mint. Add the rum and swirl the shaker to combine. Pour the drink into an imperial pint glass and fill to the top with chunky crushed ice. Garnish with a bouquet of mint sprigs, insert two straws, and drink with someone you want to touch noses with.

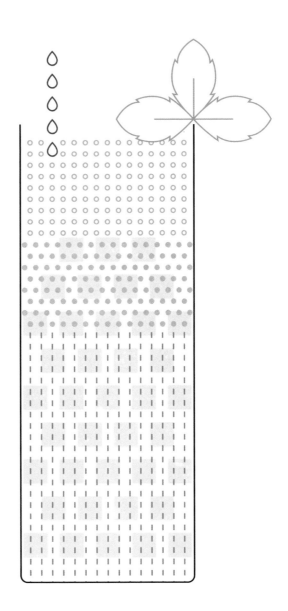

Maloney Park Swizzle

No, I did not name this for myself—Sasha named it after me. It is a riff on the Queen's Park Swizzle (pages 197 and 199). I had fallen in love with floating Peychaud's and its ability to dry a drink out without changing the texture. Also, it was so much prettier than the Angostura bitters in the original Queen's Park. We were floating fanatics back then; I have no idea who floated the first bitters on a Queen's Park or blackstrap rum on a Dark & Stormy, but he or she deserves a Nobel Prize.

—Toby Maloney

10 to 12 fresh mint leaves, plus whole sprigs for garnish
¾ oz (22 ml) fresh lime juice
¾ oz (22 ml) Simple Syrup (page 20)
2 oz (60 ml) rum, preferably Matusalem Classico
5 to 6 dashes Peychaud's bitters

Combine the mint leaves, lime juice, and simple syrup in a cocktail shaker and gently muddle. Add the rum, then transfer to a chilled Collins glass, making sure that the mint is firmly settled at the bottom of the glass. Add crushed ice to come three-quarters of the way up the sides of the glass and lightly swizzle. Float the bitters and lightly swizzle again to get a tricolor effect. Top off with more crushed ice and garnish with a bouquet of mint sprigs.

The Fix

Mojito

This is Cuba's oldest proper cocktail on record. The predecessor to the modern Mojito was a combination of mint, fresh lime, and aguardiente—a crude forerunner of rum. That drink was originally named "El Draque" in honor of Sir Francis Drake. In the mid-1800s, when the Original Bacardi company was formed, the existing El Draque recipe was changed, replacing the aguardiente with rum. And it was renamed "Mojito" after the African word mojo, which loosely translates as "to cast a little spell." This version was adapted from a recipe first served at Sloppy Joe's Bar in Havana, Cuba in 1931.

—Richard Boccato

8 to 10 fresh mint leaves, plus whole mint sprigs for garnish
1 oz (30 ml) fresh lime juice
¾ oz (22 ml) Simple Syrup (page 20)
1 brown sugar cube
2 oz (60 ml) white rum

Combine the mint, lime juice, simple syrup, and sugar cube in a cocktail shaker and gently muddle (bruise, but don't abuse!). Add the rum and pour into a chilled rocks glass. Top off with crushed ice and garnish with a bouquet of mint sprigs.

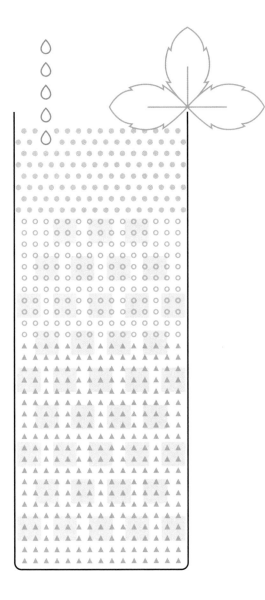

Queen's Park Swizzle (Dark)

Swizzles are traditionally made using small wooden sticks ("swizzle sticks") that are whittled from what is commonly called the Caribbean bois lélé tree. The most desirable species of these trees are found in Martinique. To swizzle means to agitate the crushed ice in a cocktail while marrying all the ingredients, so that a discernible frost forms on the outside of the glass.

This drink is both attractive and delicious. A popular variation of this cocktail, the Maloney Park Swizzle (page 193), is made with white rum and both Peychaud's and Angostura bitters, but this version is likely more similar to its original Trinidad incarnation.

—Richard Boccato

8 to 10 fresh mint leaves, plus whole sprigs for garnish
¾ oz (22 ml) Simple Syrup (page 20), made with
    Demerara sugar
1 oz (30 ml) fresh lime juice
2 oz (30 ml) overproof (or 80 proof) Demerara rum
4 to 6 dashes Angostura bitters

Combine the mint leaves, simple syrup, and lime juice in a cocktail shaker and gently muddle. Add the rum, then transfer to a chilled Collins glass, making sure that the mint is firmly settled at the bottom of the glass. Add crushed ice to come three-quarters of the way up sides of the glass and lightly swizzle. Add the bitters and lightly swizzle again to obtain a tricolor effect. Top off with crushed ice and garnish with a bouquet of mint sprigs.

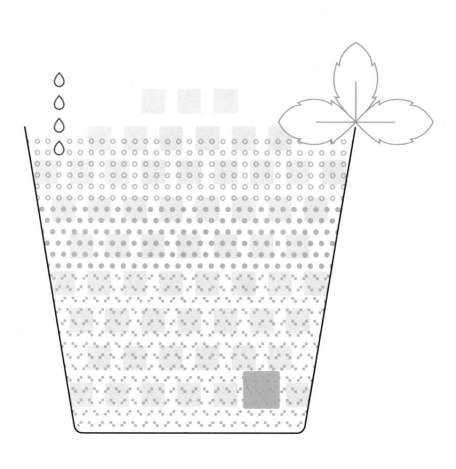

Queen's Park Swizzle (Light)

The Queen's Park Swizzle is a Mojito (page 195) with the awe-inducing addition of bitters swizzled on top. Historically the recipe calls for Angostura bitters, but at Milk & Honey we used Peychaud's bitters, which gave the drink a dramatic red visual pop on top, with the bright green mint at the bottom. This drink, quite simply, melted hearts and minds.

—Chad Solomon & Christy Pope

A handful of fresh mint sprigs, plus a whole sprig for garnish
1 brown sugar cube
1 oz (30 ml) fresh lime juice
¾ oz (22 ml) Simple Syrup (page 20)
2 oz (30 ml) white rum, preferably Flor de Caña 4 Year
4 to 5 dashes Peychaud's bitters

Combine the mint, sugar cube, lime juice, and simple syrup in a cocktail shaker and gently muddle. Add the rum and swirl to combine. Pour the cocktail into a rocks glass and add crushed ice to come to just under the rim of the glass. Add the bitters and lightly swizzle into a red layer on top of the drink, then top with more ice, shaping it into a cone. Garnish with the mint sprig (tap it on the side of your hand to release the essential oils for the optimum aroma).

The Fix

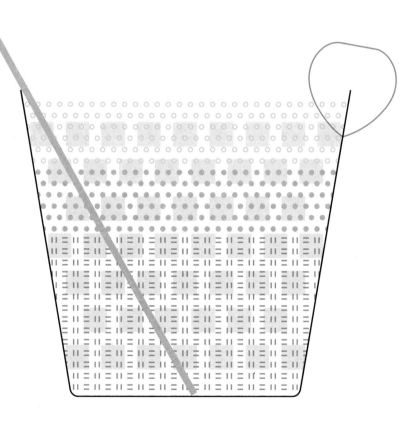

Strawberry Fix

Sasha was the king of balanced cocktails. When creating the perfect Fix or other peasant cocktails—those poured over cracked ice—it is essential to taste your citrus and syrup, as well as the fruits that will be muddled in. Sometimes the lemon is too tart, or the fruit isn't ripe enough, and you have to adjust accordingly. The key is to know what the balance should be and make the sums add up to it.

—Gil Bouhana

1 to 2 strawberries, hulled and quartered, plus 1 small
   whole strawberry for garnish
¾ oz (22 ml) fresh lemon juice
¾ oz (22 ml) Simple Syrup (page 21)
2 oz (60 ml) bourbon

Taste a piece of quartered strawberry for sweetness and tartness. Add the quartered strawberries to a chilled double rocks glass and muddle very gently to create a layer of strawberry "jam" on the bottom of the glass. Fill the glass to the top with crushed ice; set aside. Combine the lemon juice, simple syrup, and bourbon in a cocktail shaker and shake to mix. Pour over the crushed ice in the rocks glass, garnish with the whole strawberry, and serve with a straw.

Punches, Flips, and Dessert and Temperance Cocktails

Large Format Punches, Cream-Based and Sweet Cocktails, and Drinks for the Teetotaler

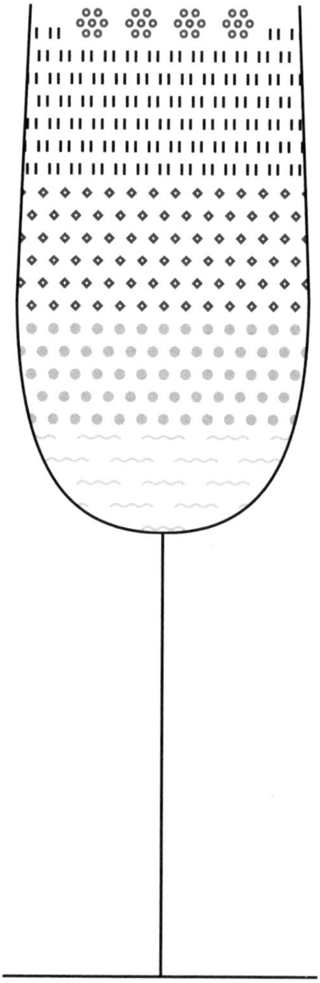

Café con Leche Flip

Sasha would savor his beloved Americanos every morning at his favorite Greenwich Village café, Doma na Rohu, as a jumpstart before making his daily lists. He described the Café con Leche Flip as that coffee—on steroids. A flip that tastes like a delicious iced coffee, this gets a power kick from the blackstrap rum.

—Sam Ross

1 oz (30 ml) Cruzan blackstrap rum
1 oz (30 ml) coffee liqueur, such as Café Lolita
¾ oz (22 ml) Simple Syrup (page 20)
¾ oz (22 ml) heavy (double) cream
1 egg yolk from a medium egg
Freshly grated nutmeg, for garnish

Combine the rum, coffee liqueur, simple syrup, cream, and egg yolk in a cocktail shaker and shake to emulsify the mixture. Fill the shaker with ice and shake vigorously until the drink is sufficiently chilled. Strain into a chilled sour glass and garnish with nutmeg.

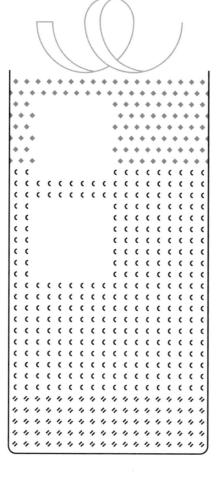

Croque M. Petraske or Croque Mme Moger

Cocktail hour in the Moger-Petraske house was a fine time of day that would span roughly between 4 p.m. and 7 p.m. The monsieur would typically say to the apron-clad madame, "Such a shame the chef is cooking without a proper libation." He would then pull two frozen highball glasses from the freezer. Sasha's go-to aperitif was a modest Campari and soda. For madame, he would add a mischievous splash of Plymouth gin.

There was usually a fruit basket in our kitchen stuffed to the gills with the previous night's bar fruit—mostly oranges without peels. This meant there was always fresh-squeezed orange juice for breakfast, but seldom any peels to garnish our cocktail hour aperitifs.

—Georgette Moger-Petraske

1½ oz (45 ml) Campari
4 oz (120 ml) club soda
1 oz (30 ml) gin, preferably Plymouth
1 orange twist, for garnish (optional)

To make the "Monsieur" cocktail, pour the Campari over 2 medium ice cubes in a frozen highball glass and top off with club soda. Stir to combine.

To make the "Madame," prepare the drink the same way, but add the gin and garnish with an orange twist, if you have one.

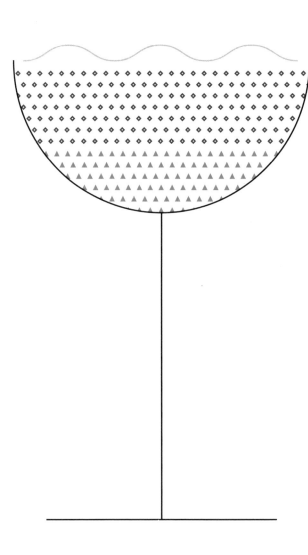

Dominicana

This was one of the first drinks Sasha created at Milk & Honey, and it was the first one he ever taught me to make. I quickly grew to respect Sasha's attention to detail and craftsmanship and have since followed the same careful process every time I work on something new. And these days, whenever I am working on a drink, I always hear Sasha's voice in the back of my head saying, "Now, increase that ingredient and decrease this one." The drink is black in color and slightly sweet, with a smooth mouthfeel. There should be a clear demarcation between the drink and the layer of cream floating on top.

—Matt Clark

1½ oz (45 ml) coffee liqueur, such as Café Lolita
1½ oz (45 ml) aged Dominican rum
Fresh whipped cream, for garnish

Add the liqueur and rum to a chilled mixing glass, fill the glass with ice, and stir until the drink is sufficiently chilled. Strain into a chilled coupe and float a thin layer of whipped cream on top.

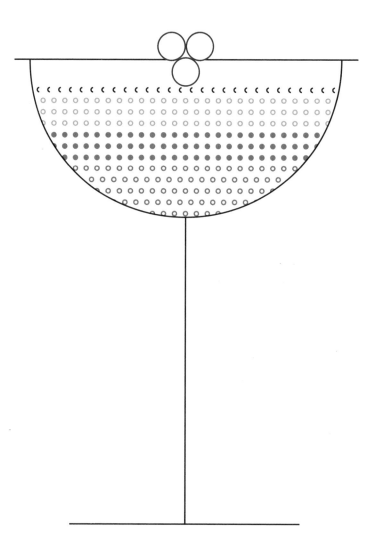

Faker Face

Served in a frosty coupe, with its beautiful frothy head and glimmering grenadine glow—by appearances, this drink's name is taken from a sobriquet given to Georgette by her father when she was a little girl pretending to be asleep in bed when it was past her bedtime.

—Luis Gil

¾ oz (22 ml) fresh lime juice
¾ oz (22 ml) grenadine syrup
1 ounce (30 ml) fresh orange juice
Club soda, for topping off
A large blackberry, for garnish

Combine the lime juice, grenadine syrup, and orange juice in an cocktail shaker filled with ice and shake vigorously until the drink is sufficiently chilled. Strain into a coupe and top off with soda. Push two toothpicks through the blackberry and balance it on the rim of the glass.

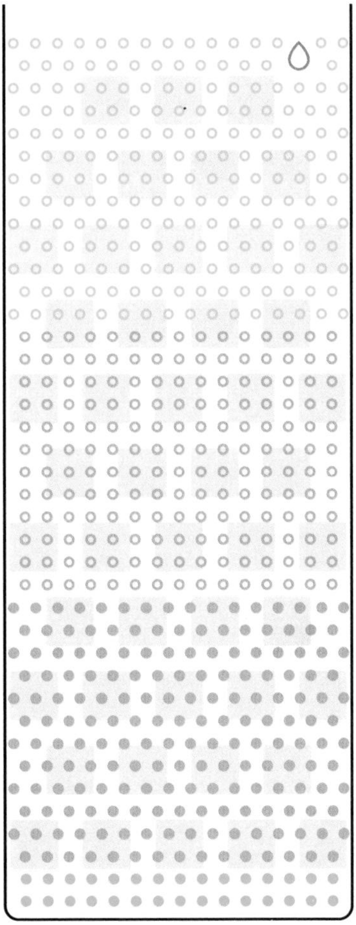

House Ginger Beer

Sasha taught a simple formula for creating libations for our teetotalers: Double up on the nonalcoholic ingredients of a cocktail to
make a base that can be modified in the same manner as a "strong"
Gimlet, Collins, Buck, or the like. For example, 1 ½ ounces (45 ml)
lemon juice, 1 ½ ounces (45 ml) simple syrup, and a soda water
topper make a delicious lemonade. Muddling mint, cucumber,
or other fruit also can be combined with club soda for a satisfying
beverage. Ginger drinks lend themselves particularly nicely to the
well of temperance cocktails, as you can make something bold and
fiery, interesting, and refreshing without alcohol.

—Abraham Hawkins

1 oz (30 ml) fresh lemon juice
1 oz (30 ml) fresh pineapple juice
1 oz (30 ml) Ginger Syrup (page 21)
1 bar spoon maple syrup
A dash of Angostura bitters
3 oz (90 ml) club soda

Combine the lemon juice, pineapple juice, ginger syrup, maple
syrup, and bitters in a mixing glass and shake vigorously. Add
the club soda and pour into a Collins glass filled with ice cubes.

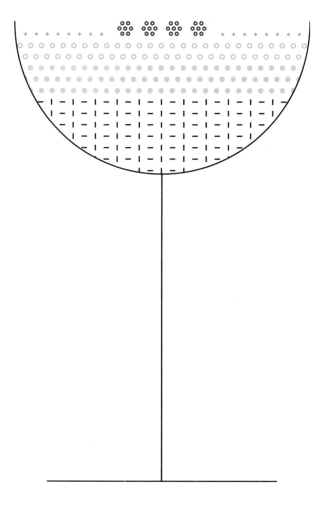

Noche Buena

This sweet dessert cocktail was the first concoction I ever put together, and I was lucky enough to have Sasha help me perfect it. Inspired by my mother, Mercedes Gil, this drink opened my mind to new cocktails.

—Carolyn Gil

½ oz (15 ml) fresh lemon juice
¾ oz (22 ml) Simple Syrup (page 20)
1½ oz (45 ml) tawny port
1 egg yolk from a medium egg
Champagne or prosecco
Freshly grated cinnamon, for garnish

Combine the lemon juice, simple syrup, port, and egg yolk in a cocktail shaker and shake to emulsify the mixture. Add a large ice cube and shake vigorously until the drink is sufficiently chilled. Strain into a chilled coupe and top off with Champagne or prosecco. Garnish with cinnamon.

Temperance Grapefruit Collins

This was Sasha's favorite drink when he stopped imbibing for a few days each month. I recall him walking around Milk & Honey with a special pitcher of double-filtered water. "You've got to try this water. Exceptional!" When he took a break from water—and spirits—the Temperance Grapefruit Collins was his standby. If you're not sticking to temperance, you could dot with three drops of Peychaud's bitters before the garnish.

—Luis Gil

1 ounce (30 ml) fresh lime juice
½ ounce (15 ml) Simple Syrup (page 20)
2 ounces (60 ml) fresh grapefruit juice
A splash of club soda, plus more for topping off
A grapefruit wedge, for garnish

Combine the lime juice, simple syrup, and grapefruit juice in a chilled cocktail shaker, add a few pebbles of ice just to chill slightly, and shake vigorously. Add the club soda, then pour into a chilled Collins glass and top off with more club soda. Garnish with the grapefruit wedge.

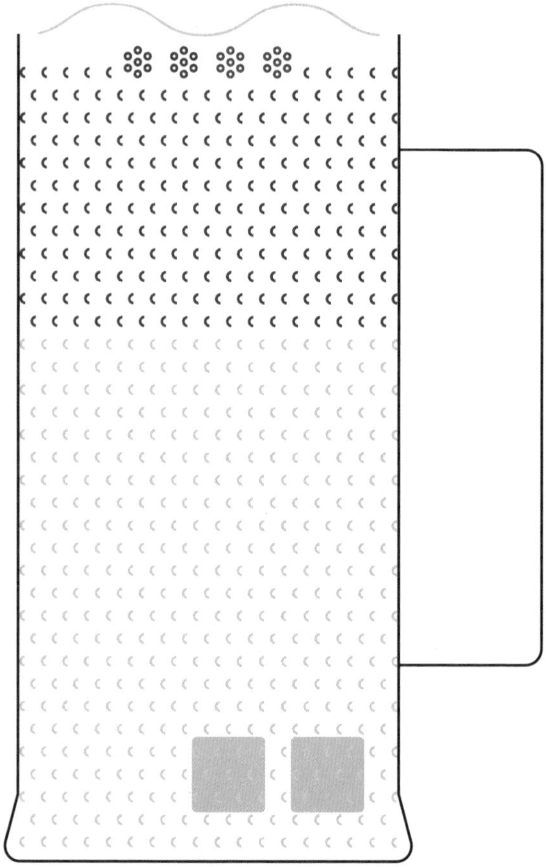

Temperance Irish Coffee

There is a photo somewhere out there of Sasha and Georgette sipping Irish Coffee at the Dead Rabbit Bar, their favorite place for it. In the photo they are both looking up with whipped-cream mustaches—Georgette in her cloche hat, Sasha in his shawl-neck cardigan—and it was one for the ages. Of course Sasha preferred his Irish coffee as a non-temperance drink, and this recipe can be altered with the addition of 1 ½ ounces (45 ml) Irish whiskey. As we didn't have a coffee maker at any of the bars, only espresso machines, we would make the drink this way.

—Eric Alperin

2 shots espresso
2 Demerara sugar cubes
Fresh whipped cream, for garnish
Freshly grated cinnamon, for garnish
Freshly grated nutmeg, for garnish

Combine the espresso and sugar cubes in an Irish coffee glass. Add 4 oz (120 ml) warm water and stir. Top with whipped cream and garnish with cinnamon and nutmeg.

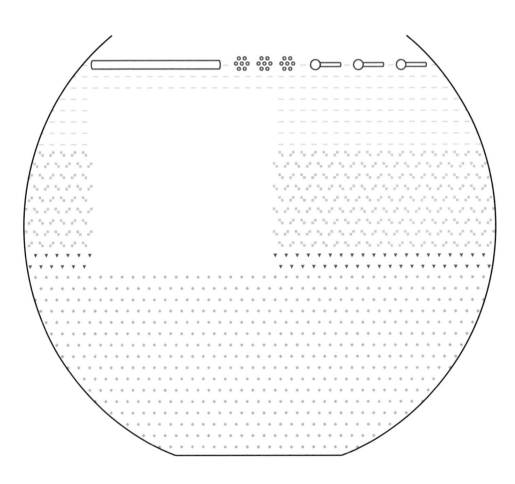

The U.S.S. Russell Punch

Named for our Brooklyn apartment on Russell Street and a nod to Sasha's Russian heritage, this cocktail was served in rambling rose-patterned teacups in the most social room of the house—the kitchen. It ensured that the party merrily rollicked along without drink requests overwhelming the bartender or the hostess.

—Georgette Moger-Petraske

Makes about 2¾ gallons (10 L), enough for a boisterous party

50 lemons, peeled and juiced
3 pounds (1 kg 360 g) granulated sugar
3 (750-ml) bottles Jamaican rum, such as Appleton's
3 (750-ml) bottles white rum, such as Flor de Cana
1 (750-ml) bottle dark rum, such as Smith & Cross
6 (750-ml) bottles prosecco
1 tablespoon freshly grated nutmeg
12 cinnamon sticks, for garnish
12 whole cloves, for garnish

Combine the lemon peels and sugar in a large punch bowl and let stand for 1½ and up to 4 hours.

Discard 80 percent of the peels from the sugar, brushing any sugar clinging to the peels back into the bowl. Add the lemon juice to the sugar; then add the Jamaican, white, and dark rums and gently whisk. Top off with 2 to 3 bottles of prosecco; add the nutmeg and whisk again. Add a 5-inch (13 cm) square block of ice and the cinnamon sticks and cloves. Refresh the punch with more prosecco over the course of the party.

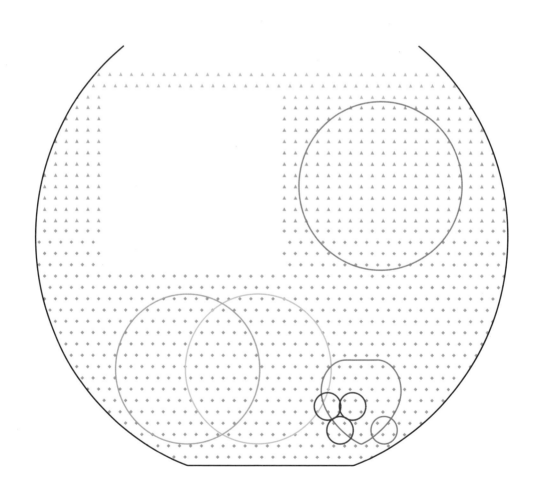

Wedding Punch

The month of May in a glass, this punch practically hums the Cole Porter songbook. Our wedding punch was a light prosecco and St-Germain refresher served in flutes that clinked like wind chimes in the garden throughout the day of our wedding.

—Georgette Moger-Petraske

Makes about 2½ gallons (10.75 L), enough for a boisterous party

1 (750-ml) bottle elderflower liqueur, such as St-Germain
4 (750-ml) bottles dry vermouth, preferably Martini bianco
8 to 10 (750-ml) bottles prosecco, depending on your preference
8 oz (230 g) assorted berries (if using strawberries,
    cut to match other berries' size)
1 orange, sliced into wheels
2 lemons, sliced into wheels
2 limes, sliced into wheels

Combine the liqueur, vermouth, and prosecco in a punch bowl large enough to hold an 8-inch (20 cm) square block of ice. Add the ice and garnish with the berries and citrus wheels.

Guides

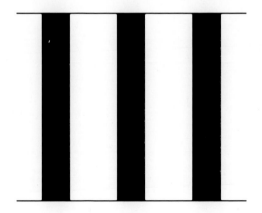

Regarding Milk & Honey House Rules (or, The Sasha Petraske Finishing School for Patrons)
By Georgette Moger-Petraske

"Why so many rules, Mr. Petraske?"
"I suppose it's because I grew up in a house without them, Miss Moger."

1. No name-dropping, no star f*cking.
2. No hooting, hollering, shouting, or other loud behavior.
3. No fighting, no play fighting, no talking about fighting.
4. Gentlemen will remove their hats. Hooks are provided.
5. Gentlemen will not introduce themselves to ladies. Ladies, feel free to start a conversation or ask the bartender to introduce you. If a man you don't know speaks to you, please lift your chin slightly and ignore him.
6. Do not linger outside the front door.
7. Do not bring anyone unless you would leave that person alone in your home. You are responsible for the behavior of your guests.
8. Exit the bar briskly and silently. People are trying to sleep across the street. Please make all your travel plans and say all farewells before leaving the bar.

The legendary house rules of Milk & Honey were more than an etiquette guide for bar decorum. They could be read as a compass for consideration of others and self-governing, drawing comparison to the *Rules of Civility & Decent Behavior in Company and Conversation*, the set of sixteenth century precepts that guided a young George Washington as a schoolboy. Though Sasha's beliefs were not from another age—graciousness, modesty, and decorum ought to be common conventions of society no matter the time. The modern cocktail bar had to be in an atrocious state when derricks were hooting, hollering, play fighting, name-dropping, and entertaining company who ran any risk of swinging from the rafters after two drinks. We can castigate, ad nauseam, the cloying cocktails and the manner in which they were served in the crepuscular days before Milk & Honey. So many of us sailing three sheets to the wind on rudderless ships navigated by misguided captains. Stormy weather, indeed.

The house rules were cast in bronze plaques on the bathroom doors of each of my husband's bars— a gentle decree from a patient chief whose sole intention was to be a good neighbor, both to those living in the building at 134 and elsewhere on Eldridge Street. The plaques were frequently stolen, as compelling a novelty as any to a thief—a coveted conversation piece for the home bar. But why? Was there any irony in a request that all business be concluded before exiting? Was it at all out of line for the host to ask that conversations not focus on the famous or infamous who might be within the room? Was the precept that gentlemen conduct themselves as such really a demand so great?

The fifty-sixth maxim contained within the *Rules of Civility* states "For 'tis better to be alone than in bad company." Circa 2000, ladies knew that a few quiet drinks spared from the company of cads and clumsy introductions were a rare commodity at any cocktail bar. In point of fact, when I read the house rule encouraging ladies to shun unwelcome advances with a slight lift of chin and volumes of silence, I made frequent dates with thick books to Milk & Honey, so frequent that Richie Boccato created a signature drink for me, the Water Lily. The reverence and hum of the Eldridge Street bar was a sanctuary of seated patrons who were required to telephone before dropping in. It was a dim den where hats were hung reverently from hooks provided. And then there were the cocktails that were served on candlelit silver trays or respectfully slid toward patrons by bartenders bound by another code of rules.

Regarding the Home Bar
by Theo Lieberman

"That's one way to do it."
— Sasha Petraske

Setting up a home bar is easier than you might think. The professional bartender relies on only a few basic tools to make outstanding drinks.

Ice: Ice from the grocery store is fine for chilling beer and wine, any pre-batched cocktails, or any 1&1 (G&T, etc.), but is not conducive for individual cocktails. While people buy special molds for large-format ice, Tupperware works just as well. Freezing a large block of ice and cutting it like a professional can be achieved with just a knife and a bar spoon. Take a medium-size Tupperware container, fill it with water, cover it, and freeze. The lid is important, because ice absorbs the flavors of the food in your freezer. Once your ice has frozen, take a standard serrated bread knife and, holding the ice in your hand (not on the counter), lightly tap it with the knife—this will cause it to split in half. Continue until you reach your desired size. Wearing painters' gloves for this can be helpful, at least in the beginning. For drinks in a Collins glass, special ice molds are sold, or just make your own ice spear roughly the length of the glass.

Jiggers: Jiggers are the best and fastest tool for measuring drinks. Look for a two-sided jigger with 1- and 2-ounce (30 and 60 ml) measures. Ideally that jigger will also have inner markings for other measurements. If not, you will also need jiggers for ¾, ½, and ¼ ounce (22, 15, and 7.5 ml, respectively) will also be needed. There are a few companies that make single jiggers with all these measurements in one. Some of these give milliliters as well as ounces. (Most pre-Prohibition cocktail books use outdated measures; as a basic rule of thumb, keep the proportions the same and then start adjusting to taste.)

Bar spoon: The longest bar spoon won't always be the most versatile. A bar spoon with a wide bowl, ideally with a disk on the top end for cracking ice, is the best. Hold the spoon in your dominant hand and the ice in the other, and tap away. This will splinter the ice. Use larger pieces for shaking drinks and smaller pieces for stirred drinks. If you're planning a party, this can be done ahead of time. Just remember to put the lid back on the container you are storing the ice in. A proper host will always have more ice than necessary set aside. A general rule of thumb is one-third to half of a bag of ice per person.

Mixing glasses: A mixing glass doesn't have to be expensive—a standard pint glass will do just fine. The most important thing to make a proper stirred up cocktail is to make sure both the mixing glass and cocktail glass are frozen. Then build your cocktail. When adding ice to a mixing glass, always use a larger piece first, as this will help you achieve the water content you are looking for with ease. Then add smaller pieces on top until the mixing glass is full. For your standard 3-ounce (90 ml) cocktail, you want to add an additional 1 ounce (30 ml) of water content from the ice. Getting the feel for how long this will be can take a bit of practice. A measuring cup and the 4-ounce (120 ml) line, will help you get a feel for it.

Cocktail strainers: There are two main types. A julep strainer should only be used for stirred drinks, whereas a Hawthorne strainer will work for both stirred and shaken cocktails. The julep strainer, which traces its name to the early days of cocktails, was meant to keep the ice and mint out of your mouth while you sipped your julep. A good Hawthorne strainer is really all you need. The key to a good strainer is not the shape or the material—but rather the coil. The tighter it is, the better the strainer. Never strain a cocktail with a tea strainer, as it will strain out too much of the drink. A small amount of citrus pulp and some fine ice crystals are what make a cocktail look alive.

Cocktail shakers: The right shaker is a personal preference. A cobbler shaker is great for a home bartender, as it is a three-piece shaker with the strainer built into the top. However, for best results, get a Boston shaker. When selecting a Boston shaker, make sure both the top and bottom pieces are metal. Cocktails should never be shaken in glass, as it won't get the drinks as cold as metal will. Also, the glass can shatter when you try to separate the metal shaker from it.

Juices and garnishes: A proper cocktail should be juiced and garnished to order. A hand juicer is best for a home bartender, as a citrus reamer won't yield as much juice and also releases too much pulp. Although it's best to juice citrus as close to the order as possible, when one entertains at home, taking care of the guests is more important. Juicing right before the party should be fine. The Hamilton Beach 932 juicer was long the preferred choice at Milk & Honey.

Garnishes should follow the same rules as juices, so they are as fresh as possible. Cut off the tips from lemons, but not from limes. The same protocol applies for prepping lemons and limes: Cut them lengthwise in half, then make a small slit on the inside about one third from the top. A garnish should never have the slice in the middle; it should appear as a flag on the side of the glass. The average lemon should yield about eight slices, and a small lime should yield about six. When it comes to oranges, cut off the tips as you would a lemon. Then place the orange on its side and cut a half inch out of its center. This will remove the inside slices that are not pleasing to see or to eat.

Citrus twists must always be done to order as their oils are subject to oxidation. Learning how to use a good Swiss peeler will prove a most useful skill.

Cucumbers may be sliced ahead of time at home, although in a good cocktail bar, it's best done to order. When muddling cucumbers, remember that too much force will bruise the vegetable, and it can become bitter.

Fruit is always best when in season. If you don't care to eat it, don't put it in your drink.

Glassware: The two most important things to keep in mind are the size of the glass and the temperature. Serving a cocktail in a warm glass means you don't care. If you can't find room in your freezer to chill your glasses, fill each one with ice and water to cool. This is especially important with shaken and stirred cocktails that will be served up in coupes. Tall and rocks cocktails give you a bit more room for error. If you are struggling for freezer space, anything that will be built in the glass (e.g., Old Fashioned, Negroni, etc.) can go into a room-temperature glass. The additional water content that will be added to the cocktail via the ice cubes is actually desirable in this case. This is why we do not stir cocktails that will be served on the rocks in a mixing glass. Do keep this in mind when you ice the cocktail during the round of drinks you are making.

Regarding Style
by Michael Arenella

"A gentleman should always carry on his person a card listing the measurements of his intended, in the event he passes something for her in the shop windows."

– Sasha Petraske

My family descended from European immigrants who came to the United States in the the early twentieth century. Though impoverished, they still dressed like aristocrats in public. Even those with the most humble means carried an aura of dignified refinement, which was reflected in their attire. It was aspirational to dress above your financial station, and I'd imagine it helped them along by bettering the lens through which they were perceived as they struggled up the ladder toward a better life.

From the most subversive characters, anarchists and criminals; to bohemians (artists, writers, and musicians); and on to the upper citizens of society, such as bankers and lawyers—it would be difficult to discern their class at first glance, because wearing a suit was the way any grown man was expected to dress. For men, the suit was the ultimate equalizer, and it went a long way toward breaking down class structure. It almost compelled you to achieve the American dream, to become what you were dressed for and wanted to be.

At a certain point in American history, though, a mania surrounding "casual comfort" came about. Looking as if you had enough money not to care about the way you dressed became the look of success, and the suit was relegated to either corporate culture or, on the other end, uniformed public servants. Either way, the suit became an emblem of conformity, greed, and structure—a relic. Sadly, this precipitated a breakdown of culture. Manners, chivalry, and decorum were compromised, and masculine style took a turn back toward boyhood.

The good news is that in recent years, I have noticed youth culture tiring a bit of this casual mania. The cues of classic style have made a reprise in popular culture. Classic cocktails, clothing, music, and romance are seeing a renaissance.

Regarding Travel
by Georgette Moger-Petraske

"No time like the present, Miss Moger."
"No present like time, Mr. Petraske."

Sasha kept a constantly evolving mental record of how to travel with decorum. On subways: The elderly and pregnant were priorities, and no man should ever sit before every woman who wishes to rest has been offered a seat. On walking: Lady on the inside, man on the outside. And a gentleman carries with him two handkerchiefs—one for himself and one for a woman passing by in tears. (This, Sasha insisted, was inevitable in New York City.) On airplane travel: "In an emergency, I would likely be the last person out of the plane, having made sure everyone, including those stampeding to the exits, was ushered to safety."

In a letter, he once mused, "Traveling on Saturday is surely the poor man's first class." He would also say the same of the Amtrak dining car, where there was plenty of room to stretch out and indulge in the *Economist* (him) and *The New York Times* (me), or draw up bar plans (him) and polish overdue articles (me). "The gentleman will carry the bags. The lady, the cocktails." An endearing, optimistic creed if ever there were; it was a given that the gentleman would only narrowly make the train, and the lady was often left finding clever ways to maneuver her overnight luggage and several rounds of on-board cocktails.

For consideration: the 2.0 solution—a petite 6¾-ounce (200 ml) bottle of Pellegrino Pompelmo Sparkling, with 2 ounces (60 ml) removed from it and replaced with 2 ounces (60 ml) Plymouth gin. If more time and portable containers were to be found, our Croque Monsieur and Madame variations (page 207) would be readied for the rails: Monsieur with his "ham and cheese" of Campari and soda, and Madame in similar suit, with gin acting as the "egg."

Regarding Charity
by Georgette Moger-Petraske

"Generosity and a dégagé view towards even irreplaceable objects are the very things I have always held dear."

—Sasha Petraske

My husband's moral compass was set to coordinates most people would view as extreme. For me, it was one of his most endearing qualities, and I aspired to have ours align as often as possible. Sasha cared little for material possessions, and despite appearing ever dapper in crisp suits, he actually had very few clothes. Concurrent with the season, it was usually the same suit—alternating neckties as a sleight of hand. I recall him reaching for the tuxedo he wore on our honeymoon the morning he realized he had run out of clean clothes, just before we were to host a few friends for brunch. He answered the door to our guests in a bowtie and spats while I played along upstairs, juicing oranges in an evening gown.

Sasha came with little other than some very complicated bar tools when we set up our home—which was a surprise, considering how learned he was in the categories of Russian literature, world history, and rare pre-Prohibition cocktail tomes. Where I cherished the page scent and feel of a first edition, he thrilled that the same book could be read in a weightless edition before being forever cast into the ethers with a swoop of the finger. He aimed to be the opposite of the Tim O'Brien novel *The Things They Carried*; Sasha was more along the lines of *The Things He Gave Away*. Beyond possessing a lack of holdfast for even the most sentimental material object, what mattered most to my husband was that human need was met before frivolous indulgence. "We will always live comfortably and have enough for ourselves," he told me before we were married, "but we will never be rich. The money that would classify us as wealthy would be given to those in greatest need before we were ever put in the category of spendthrifts." As newlyweds, we were still far from a state of easy living, but Sasha was a master at laying down sets of preemptive self-governed rules, and for the most part, they were things that we could all serve to take a cue from.

Many of Sasha's personal rules were rooted in improving himself to being the best he could be. "Being early is not a waste of time," "Eat before you are starving," and "Remember things always take longer than you think they will," were just a few items on the to-do lists that he printed up and then crossed off every day. Rules about gentlemen keeping to any deal made on a handshake and a successful business model being one that sought a way to give back to the community were a given. As Sasha watched the craft cocktail movement evolve into a multibillion dollar industry, he saw that there was much room for corporations and individual representatives to help out the less fortunate, whose larger concern might be how to afford heart surgery for their infant, rather than being a spectator of the Ziegfeld-level follies celebrating, for example, the Negroni.

It was this that prompted him to co-found the not-for-profit, weeklong event, the San Antonio Cocktail Conference. Sasha loved the history and antiquity of San Antonio, Texas. He loved its neighborliness. "You could build a bar there and, rather than have a community board seeking to find ways of preventing it from opening, you're more likely to have your landlord help you figure out the logistics of air conditioning the place."

The San Antonio Cocktail Conference partnered with Houston Street Charities, and, ensured that 100 percent of the profits were divided among selected children's charities. Its slogan: Pouring Our Hearts Out.

"Sasha was fascinated by the idea of conferences and how they could advance the craft. Immediately he hit on how it would best come together. A worthy beneficiary would be needed; he didn't want to have anything to do with it unless there was a charity involved," said cofounder Scott Becker. "Sasha believed that should be the heart and soul of the marketing endeavor, to be involved in the community." Sasha and Scott worked in their first year with HeartGift, an existing nonprofit. "By SACC's third year, we were able to benefit two children's charities, and in the fourth year, four of them: HeartGift, ChildSafe, Transplants for Children, and The Children's Shelter."

Scott Becker added, "Houston Street Charities would not have become the success it is without Sasha's indefatigable commitment to the cause. He believed it was our responsibility to give back. An established person and brand owes it to the community they come to with these festivals to get involved. It's a business model that very few businesses understand."

Regarding Posture and Etiquette
by Eric Alperin

"As Benjamin Frankin said, 'Beauty is five percent
skincare and ninety-five percent spinal alignment,'
or something to that effect, anyway."

—Sasha Petraske

I would witness Sasha talking to tables by getting down to their level. He wasn't the most comfortable in social settings, and I have to believe that is what gave him the understanding of what it meant to really serve as purposeful in a room full of people. Standing at a table looking down at your guests was a position that Sasha would feel uncomfortable in. What to do? Get on the same level.

Sasha had spent time in boot camp as a U.S. Army Ranger. When he told me this, it made me think that he had learned to train his body to adjust to the most effective position he could be in for whatever the situation. Or, maybe the physical forms forced onto him in the Army became survival techniques by which he protected himself in uncomfortable social settings.

He taught us all to hold any piece of glassware at its lowest point. Who will ever forget the image of Sasha standing at attention while holding a coupe at its base? Or that during service, when your hand might graze your face or you might run your fingers through your hair, you would immediately run to the sink and wash your hands? Your hands were tools to execute your craft with a sense of etiquette.

Sasha's body always seemed to be at perfect attention in the most available way, while striving not to be a physical obstacle or nuisance. Core strength was so very important to him, as it involved the muscles that propagated good eating, biking, and writing postures. At a restaurant and want the check? Sit upright in check-sitting posture! Almost always when I witnessed this ninja move in action, a server appeared.

When Sasha visited Los Angeles to work on The Varnish, I saw that he finally was able to find a bit more time for hiking, yoga, and green juices. When he was training staff in Austin for the Half Step, he had seen a TED Talk on power poses, so the following day, the session with the staff was all about finding your own power pose.

As children, we learn viscerally through our bodies, which then inform our minds. Sasha to me was the "forever child" with a playfully informed sense of etiquette and posture. He was always more interested in conversation when he was learning from others than in talking about himself, and in the end his search for answers was a celebration.

Regarding How to Be a Good Bar Regular
by David Wondrich

"Good manners are the hallmark of a gentleman."

—Sasha Petraske

Human ambition takes many forms. The people I've known, however, who have set their hearts on becoming regulars at one great bar or another are generally in it for the long haul. To be a true regular is a noble thing, and it requires time and effort. To be one takes much more than coming in repeatedly, sitting at the bar, and spending money. It takes acceptance — acceptance from the bartenders and the other people who work in the bar, but also, and just as important, acceptance by the other regulars.

To gain that acceptance, you have to make yourself useful to each group, and that takes some knowledge and some skill. But once it's gained, that kind of acceptance is worth a great deal in this cold, hustling world of ours. You will find it all in Sasha's Milk & Honey House Rules (page 226). If you've got those internalized, you'll be a good regular. That said, I'd still like to mention a couple of things I've learned from almost forty years of drinking in bars.

Don't be a hog. If you spend a lot of time in a bar, you (hopefully) will get to know the bartenders. Bartenders in great bars are often great people, or at least fun to talk to. One of the pleasures of being a regular is talking to them. But when things are busy and you start telling Allie about this funny thing that happened to you, it puts her in a bit of a jam. On the one hand, you're a good customer, she finds you amusing, and she doesn't want to be rude and cut you off. On the other, there are twenty other people waiting for drinks. Save the story for when it's slow. Likewise, your quest to try different versions of the Sidecar until you find one that's perfect? Fun on a Monday night. On a Thursday, it's an imposition. Regulars have access; true regulars don't abuse it — after all, they'll be back.

Pitch in. I'm not saying you should try to do anyone else's job. But if the joint is busy, and on the way to the bathroom you notice empty glasses piling up around the place, why not pick a few of them up on the way back and bring them to the bar? Or, if the place prides itself on its extensive vodka collection and you find yourself in, say, Kyrgyzstan, why not pick up a bottle of Kyrgyz vodka for the bar? I'm not saying you can bribe your way into regulardom — this isn't something you want to overdo, because then it imposes an obligation, and obligations are a drag.

Don't pimp out your status as a regular. So, you know the bartenders by name and have tried every drink on the list. You're comfortable there, and you want to share that comfort with your friends. That's excellent—bars need customers. But this might not be the place to have the reunion of your sorority drinking team. If you introduce your friends to the bar, they'd better be the sort who go with the place, or at least who aren't going to put dings in the other customers' good times. In other words, being a regular is not something you show off. Likewise, it doesn't entitle you to anything at all. Just because the bartender has given you a buyback in the past or the kitchen has sent out a basket of popcorn shrimp doesn't mean they have to do it this time. It's not your entitlement. And if they do it, don't forget to tip.

Listen more than you speak. Any bar's regulars are a community, and if you want to join it, you'd best learn its rules—which are, of course, unwritten and usually unspoken. Eventually you can start talking. But even though you know everyone there and see them all the time, they're not your therapy group. Best to leave the deep personal problems at home.

You can also talk to strangers, of course—part of a regular's job (or is it a calling?) is to minister to the new and confused. You don't want to overdo it. But nice, well-behaved types who are a bit puzzled by the lack of Scotch in this bourbon bar or by why the bartender keeps calling them "Mike" (he calls everyone Mike)? You can clue them in. And if they prove civilized, you can even rope them into the general conversation—that's how new regulars are made.

But really. Just follow Sasha's rules.

Regarding Milk & Honey
Comp Protocol
by Sasha Petraske

"If you're serious about making cocktails at home, the first thing you have to do is take all the food out of your freezer and throw it away. It'll add unwanted flavor to the ice, and you weren't going to eat it anyway".

—Sasha Petraske

Below you will find the industry's most liberal staff drinks and complimentary drink policy. Milk & Honey has always run on the Honor System, with no inventory controls, managers, camera, or evil, potentially self-aware and murderous POS machines. The Honor System, we have found, brings Honor to all concerned. Honor, and fewer Terminators.

In 2005, Mr. Joseph Schwartz and I were, I believe, alone in the industry in believing that, with enough training and setup, relatively young men and women can provide the highest level of service without a salaried authority figure who does little to contribute to the actual work. At every high-end, high-presentation venue, one finds a Manager in a suit, there to supervise, prevent theft and waste, and represent the owners to the customers, over the heads of the staff, as an adult in the case of conflict or complaint. The Floor Manager in most bars and lounges draws a salary most likely larger than the theft he might prevent, symbol that the owner doesn't trust the staff. Joseph and I set out to create a Manager-less Bar.

Our policy's length and breadth makes it crucial that it actually be followed. There is no financial space to give any more than what is described below. Our high retail markup gives us the room to give away the many and many types of free cocktails that are needed to water the garden that Harry Craddock alluded to in the cover inscription of *The Savoy Cocktail Book*.

The shockingly low liquor cost we run gives us this room, but barely. New York's history is full of bars that went bankrupt even as they were packed six nights a week. As tipped employees, you are paid a literal percentage of the business's gross, but need not contribute to the cost of the stock. A bar that gives away too many quality ingredients can bleed to death in front of one's eyes.

Staff may drink during service, but not enough to raise the blood alcohol level to 0.08. A breathalyzer is provided. A bartender or waiter in a cocktail bar is legally and morally responsible for the safety of the people she or he serves. Decisions about services of alcohol and estimations of the sobriety of a given guest cannot be made by an inebriated person.

That being said, cocktail bartenders drink cocktails. A bartender who prefers a beer and a shot to a cocktail while at work is a bit like an acupuncturist who wants to go to a Western doctor when she is sick. It demonstrates a lack of faith in one's own medicine. Such bartenders tend to make unbalanced and overly complicated original cocktails. If there is a social imperative to toast with a customer, it is permissible to drink a one-ounce portion of neat spirit, preferably an amaro, rather than a shot from a bottle of 90-proof rye that we have trouble finding six months of the year. The point of the staff drinking policy is to make one constantly investigate and improve one's craft, not to give your already cool job the most affluent perks available.

Girlfriends, Boyfriends, Spouses, Parents, etc., will not be charged for alcohol, so long as they can carry it without inconveniencing the patrons. Food will be charged at the staff discount or comped if it is perishable.

Roommates, Friends, Ex-Girlfriends, etc., may have up to one free drink and one free one-ounce shot, and may not tip at all, no exceptions. They must be charged for anything past this, on your honor. Note that a regular customer that you are friendly with but only socialize with at the bar is not in this category.

Celebrities, Food Journalists, Brand Ambassadors, Liquor/Wine/Beer Saleswomen, Bloggers, Politicians (including Community Board Members), and anyone seated with them are not given any free drinks unless it is to correct our error.

Upstairs, immediately adjacent, and directly-across-the-street neigh-bors will be offered a half-size free drink or one free one-ounce shot, and should tip.

Anyone with a cat on his shoulder (but not a dog or a bird) gets one free drink; the cat gets a bowl of milk.

Schoolteachers, Firefighters, Active-Duty Military, Senior Citizens over the age of 75, and single women or couples dressed, for real, like it's before the Second World War (I'm talking Boardwalk Empire level of dressed up) get one free drink, and should tip.

Paying customers should be charged for every drink they order unless it is to make up for slow service or other mistakes on our part, or, of course, Bartender's Choice drinks that are not to the customer's taste. Drinks to encourage repeat business and healthy tipping should be sent with our compliments, in portion sizes half the usual amount. Staff has complete discretion to send one (and only one) per customer.

Thought should be given to the guest's safety as far as the drink's ABV, and to timing as far as turning tables when guests are waiting. Base spirits that cost the house more than thirty dollars per 750 ml bottle should not be used except in the rarest of cases. Perishable wines can be comped at last call if there is only one glass left. Unless the guest requests it specifically, our bottled beers should be avoided as a comp, as this costs us three times what a shot costs.

Regarding Cocktails for Your Cat
by Sasha Petraske

Now, let me assuage any fears my readers may have and forestall any angry letters being written at this very moment. We are not going to be giving any alcohol to any cats. Some small amounts of *Nepeta cataria*, or common catnip, perhaps. No alcohol, however. So, when we say "Cat Cocktails," what we mean are Cat Treats, small amounts of food in the form of foam or occasionally liquid. The category of solid cat treats must be properly called cat hors d'oeuvres, and should be addressed in another volume.

It may seem a bit crazy to purchase more than one type of little saucer for the Cat Cocktails we will be creating. However, some people might find the whole idea of making cocktails for cats crazy in and of itself. As these people are plainly close-minded and ignorant, I would hesitate to cast aspersions on the sanity of anyone who wanted to go to town on crockery in this case. For my regal creatures Maggie and Anoushka, however, only one type is just fine.

Milk & Honey
Closing Night Menu

It was half-past five when Sasha and I ushered out what was to be Milk & Honey's very last patron. The strike of the bolt sounded a clarion of finality, one of regret and relief. I took my intended's hand into the corridor and we danced cheek to cheek, the Ink Spots' "Every Night About This Time" crackling through the hall. Champagne saucers sat sipped clean at every booth, highballs with diamonds of ice shimmered in pools of condensation. The blue hour of morning slipped a peal of white light through the hall, a soft spill of penumbra paid no mind. We made the executive decision to clean up nothing. We just waltzed out of there on love's languid cloud and went to breakfast at the Lyric Diner. There would always be tomorrow.

—Georgette Moger-Petraske

Index

Sasha Petraske opened Milk & Honey, a speakeasy cocktail bar in New York, in 2000. He later had ventures in New York, Los Angeles, London, and Melbourne—and was the co-founder of the San Antonio Cocktail Conference. Sasha and his bars won numerous international competitions and awards. He lived in New York until his untimely death in 2015. Georgette Moger-Petraske is a spirits writer and is the wife of the late Sasha Petraske.

Georgette Moger-Petraske wishes to gratefully acknowledge her mother and father and her loyal writing companion, Anoushka the cat. Further gratitude to Ann-Eliza Taylor, Amy Wright, the Petraske family, Aunt June Rose, the Phaidon family, Gale and Lynn Tidwell, Susan Kostrzewa, Kara Newman, Robert Simonson, Kristan and Kirby Farmer and our Hudson family, the Gil Family, Evie and the Doma family, TJ Siegal (for being a dear friend to Sasha), Kelly Chang, Nicole Casanova, Joanie Ellen and Alex Klein, Nelli and Jim Black, Eric Alperin, Julie Reiner and Susan Fedroff, Audrey Saunders, the Little and Middle Branch Families, the Attaboys, John Bonsignore, Britt Kubat, Karla Brown, Hanna Lee and Michael Anstendig, Richard MacWilliams, Kimberly Forrest and the La Mer family, Aaron Bloom, Andres and Kara Small, Nicholas Russotto, Bao Ong, Meg Strecker, M. Ward, Kiki Lenoue and Greg Tormo, the Desmonds, the Walston family, the Hotel Elysée family, the 21 Club family, the John Dory family, Alan Segan, Richie and Paty Boccato and the Dutch Kills family, Scott Becker and our San Antonio family, and all of the talented, dedicated bartenders whose passion for their craft and love of their Chief helped make this book possible.

Phaidon Press Limited
Regent's Wharf
All Saints Street
London N1 9PA

Phaidon Press Inc.
65 Bleecker Street
New York, NY 10012

phaidon.com
First published 2016
Reprinted 2017 (twice)
© 2016 Phaidon Press Limited

ISBN 9780714872810

A CIP catalogue record for this book is available from the British Library and the Library of Congress.
All rights reserved.

No part of this publication may be reproduced, stored in a retrieval system or transmitted, in any form or by any means, electronic, mechanical, photocopying, recording or otherwise, without the written permission of Phaidon Press Limited.

Commissioning Editor:
Emily Takoudes

Project Editor:
Olga Massov

Production Controller:
Matthew Harvey

Design and Illustrations:
Studio Lin

Phaidon would like to thank the following people for their contributions: Evelyn Battaglia, Kate Slate, Judith Sutton, Abraham Hawkins, Ben Long, Carolyn Gil, Chad Solomon, Christy Pope, Dale DeGroff, Danny Gil, David Wondrich, Eric Alperin, Georgette Moger-Petraske, Gil Bouhana, Jose Gil, Joseph Schwartz, Karin Stanley, Lauren McLaughlin, Lucinda Sterling, Luis Gil, Marcos Tello, Matt Clark, Michael Arenella, Michael Madrusan, Richie Boccato, Robert Simonson, Sam Ross, Theo Lieberman, Toby Maloney, Vincenzo Errico, and Zachary Gelnaw-Rubin.

Printed in China